The
MEREHURST
Cake
Decorator

MEREHURST
LONDON

Published 1990 by Merehurst Limited,
Ferry House, 51/57 Lacy Road,
London SW15 1PR

First published in 1988 by Leisure
Magazines, 46 Egerton Road,
Silverwater, NSW 2141, Australia

© Leisure Magazines

ISBN: 1 85391 065 1

Editor: Alison Leach
Typeset by Avocet Robinson,
Buckingham
Printed in Belgium by Proost
International Book Production

Front cover shows *Peach Engagement
Cake*. The doves and inscription are
piped on the top; the sides are finished
with ribbon insertion, embroidered
bows and flowers. Silk flowers are
assembled on top.
From *The Art of Sugarcraft: Sugar
Flowers* by Nicholas Lodge, published
by Merehurst.

Notes
In all the recipes, quantities are given
in metric, imperial and cups. It is
important to follow only one set of
measures as these are not
interchangeable. All spoon measures are
level.
   Eggs used in the recipes are medium
(ie, Size 3 in the UK).
   Ovens should be preheated to the
specified temperatures.
   American readers should replace the
given quantities of vanilla essence with
pure vanilla extract to taste.

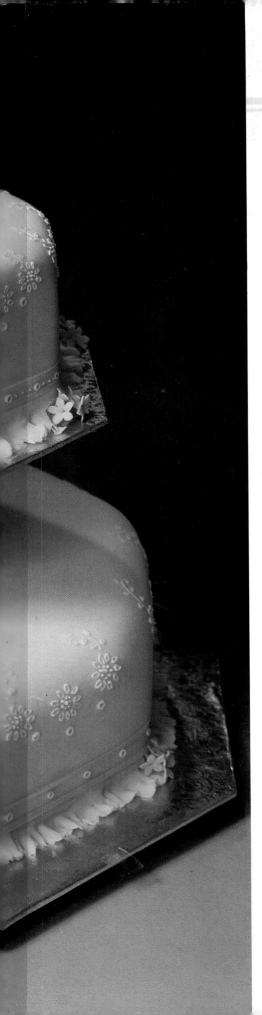

INTRODUCTION

Whether you are already an experienced cake decorator on the look out for new ideas and advanced techniques or a beginner needing to learn the simple basic techniques, this book will be a source of inspiration.

The beautiful wedding cake looks most impressive and the accompanying step-by-step photographs and instructions show you how to achieve such a result with confidence. The christening cake is decorated with a charming combination of alphabet boxes and moulded animals; again, full instructions are provided.

To emphasize the international interest in cake decorating, two cakes made for celebrations in France and Sicily are also featured.

In the section on how to win cake decorating competitions you will discover how the judges award marks. You may well recognize some of your own past mistakes! In any case you will be reminded of the importance of every detail from covering the board neatly to achieving a well-balanced design.

If you do not have the time or patience to ice cakes elaborately, you will find the ideas for instant cake decoration invaluable. The marzipan fruits are also quite quick and easy to make.

Children will enjoy making the gingerbread shapes to hang on the Christmas tree and will probably think of some weird and wonderful designs for the Easter eggs.

As chocolate is irresistible to most people, a tempting selection of recipes from many countries for rich and luscious cakes has been included, with some helpful advice on working with chocolate. There are also recipes for rich fruit cakes with a chart showing how to calculate quantities of ingredients for different sizes and shapes of tins.

If you would like to know more about cake decorating, Merehurst have a very comprehensive list of other titles on this creative activity.

CONTENTS

MARZIPAN FRUITS

Marzipan fruits look wonderful when used to
decorate cakes, or they can be eaten as petits fours
with coffee after dinner. On the following pages
you will see how easy they are to make.

M any people claim they do not like marzipan, but it is usually the taste of almond essence that they object to. If you would like to make marzipan fruits, for example, but do not like the taste of almond essence, then leave it out. Brandy or vanilla essence will do just as well.

To make 500 g (1 lb) marzipan
250 g (8 oz, 2¼ cups) ground almonds
250 g (8oz, 1½ cups) icing (confectioner's) sugar
10 ml (2 tsp) lemon juice
10 ml (2 tsp) brandy or sherry
few drops of almond essence, optional
2 small egg whites
extra icing sugar

Step 1

Mix together the ground almonds and icing sugar in a bowl. Add lemon juice, brandy or sherry and almond essence if using.

Step 2

Add the egg whites (unbeaten), a little at a time, until you have a paste that is sticky but not wet.

Step 3
Dust a board with extra icing sugar and knead the marzipan until it is smooth.

Step 4
Form into a log shape, wrap in plastic wrap and store in the refrigerator. It will keep for 4 weeks.

PAINTING FRUITS

Marzipan fruits should be moulded into shape and left to dry in a cool place, but not in the refrigerator, for 24 hours before painting. They can then be covered and stored in the refrigerator for 1 week. Marzipan fruits are painted with food colourings, either diluted or undiluted, depending upon the result you want. Use fine, good quality paintbrushes.

APPLES

Form the marzipan into small balls, slightly flattening the base and top. Make a hole in the top with a clove and use either a clove or a piece of real cherry stalk as the apple stalk. Using a paintbrush, paint some apples with red food colouring, some with green.

GRAPES

To make a bunch of grapes, form marzipan into nine tiny balls, stick them together pyramid fashion and use a clove as the stalk. Paint them with mauve or green food colouring.

WATERMELON SLICES

Form marzipan into small balls and flatten them into circles. Cut each circle in half and allow to dry. Paint the curved edge with green good colouring, leave a tiny strip of natural-coloured marzipan and paint the remainder with pink food colouring. When it has dried, paint on seeds with brown food colouring.

CHERRIES

Form marzipan into tiny balls and use a clove to make a hole in the top of each one. Cut a vanilla bean into long slivers, bend each one in two and insert each end into a cherry to form pairs. As the vanilla bean dries, it stiffens. Paint the cherries with red food colouring.

PEARS

Roll pieces of marzipan into a ball and then mould into pear shapes. Insert a piece of real pear stalk, cherry stalk or a clove into the top and when dry, paint with yellow food colouring. Shading is achieved by using both diluted and undiluted yellow food colouring.

SIMPLE TECHNIQUES
LINING THE TIN

Cake tins (pans) are lined with paper to protect the cake while it is baking. Rich fruit cakes can become too brown on the outside while the centre can still be uncooked. A paper-lined tin also ensures that the cooked cake has the even surface necessary as a base for a smooth finish of fondant.

Greaseproof (wax) and brown paper are the materials most used to line tins. Depending on the quality and thickness of the paper used, one or two layers of brown and two or three of greaseproof are usual for an average-sized cake. With larger tins and longer cooking times, more layers are needed.

Lining paper should be about 7.5 cm (3 in) higher than the tins. Try to cut all the layers at once so that they are exactly the same size. Some decorators like to oil the sheets of paper lightly to make them more manageable, but this is not essential.

Lining a square or rectangular cake tin

To line a square or rectangular tin, cut out paper 6 cm (2½ in) longer and wider than the combined measurements of the base and two sides. Eg for a 20 cm (8 in) square tin with 7.5 cm (3 in) sides, cut paper 41 cm (16½ in) square. For a rectangular tin 20 × 15 cm (8 × 6 in) with 7.5 cm (3 in) sides, cut paper 41 × 36 cm (16½ × 14½ in).

Place the tin exactly in the centre of the paper and mark around the base with a sharp pencil. Put the tin to one side, crease the paper along the pencil lines and cut paper at each corner at right angles. Shape the paper into a box with the short flaps positioned on the outside. Put the paper into the tin and make sure that it fits snugly into the corners.

Lining a round cake tin

To line a round tin, place the tin on paper and mark around the base with a sharp pencil. Use scissors to cut out the rounds. Then cut some paper in a long strip 6 cm (2½ in) wider than the height of the tin and 10 cm (4 in) longer than the circumference. Fold a margin of 3 cm (1¼ in) along one edge and slash the paper at regular intervals with scissors. Ease the paper into the tin, flattening the slashed paper so it lies flat on the base of the tin. Place the rounds of paper on top.

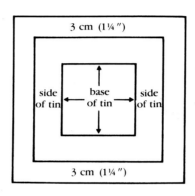

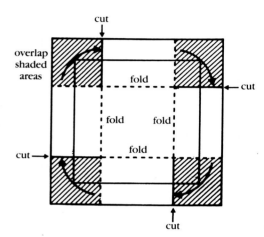

Lining a square or rectangular tin
1. Cut paper 6 cm (2½ in) longer and wider than combined measurements of base and two sides.
2. Cut paper and fold in shaded areas.

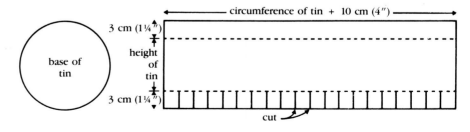

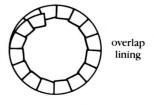

Lining a round tin
1. Cut paper exact size of tin.
2. For sides, cut paper 6 cm (2½ in) wider than height of side and 10 cm (4 in) longer than circumference of tin. Slash bottom edge.
3. Overlap slashed edge to fit curve of tin neatly.

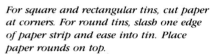

For square and rectangular tins, cut paper at corners. For round tins, slash one edge of paper strip and ease into tin. Place paper rounds on top.

Shape the paper into a box with the short flaps on the outside. Ease into tin and make sure it fits snugly into the corners.

COVERING THE BASE BOARD

A perfectly prepared
base board covered with
paper or fabric always
enhances the appearance
of any decorated cake.

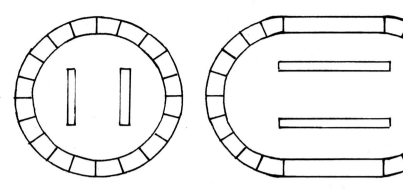

Base boards for cakes are available from all cake decorating suppliers. They are sold both covered with paper or plain. Most do not have cleats or runners underneath and it is a good idea to add these to give support and ease of lifting. Runners are made from lengths of 1-cm (½-in) wide dressed timber and are glued or tacked on. Base boards may be made from hardboard or plywood by any handy person. Thick cardboard is unsuitable as it can bend and buckle and ruin a finished cake.

To cover a square or rectangular board

Put the top of the board on the under-side of the paper. Mark the shape of the board with a sharp pencil. Cut out allowing a 5-cm (2-in) margin all around from the pencil line. Spread a thin layer of glue all over the paper and place a little on the board as well. Smooth the paper on to the board and make sure there are no trapped air bubbles or wrinkles. Turn the board over and trim the corners. Carefully fold down the margin on to the board and press down firmly. If liked, the under-sides of the boards can also be covered. Cut paper to fit around the runners and then glue paper into place.

To cover a round or oval board

Put the top of the board on the under-side of the paper. Mark the shape of the board with a sharp pencil and cut out, allowing a 5-cm (2-in) margin all around. Slash the paper with scissors at regular intervals to the pencil line. Spread adhesive all over the paper and place a little on the board as well. Smooth paper on to the board and make sure there are no trapped air bubbles or any wrinkles. Turn board over and fold the slashed margin, neatly overlapping it.

Round
Cut covering 5 cm (2 in) larger than board. Slash margin at 1.5-cm (¾-in) intervals before applying glue. Overlap slashed paper for neat edge.

Oval
Cut covering 5 cm (2 in) larger than base board. Slash margin at 1.5-cm (¾-in) intervals before applying glue. Overlap slashed paper for neat edge.

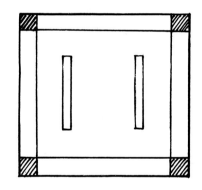

Square
Cut covering 5 cm (2 in) larger than base board. Trim corners of excess paper before applying glue. Fold glued margin on to board.

Heart
Cut covering 5 cm (2 in) larger than base board. Slash margin at 1.5-cm (¾-in) intervals and trim away excess paper at point before applying glue. Overlap slashed paper for neat edge.

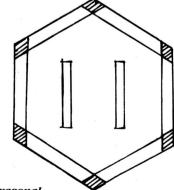

Hexagonal
Cut covering 5 cm (2 in) larger than base board. Trim corners of excess paper before applying glue. Fold glued margin on to board.

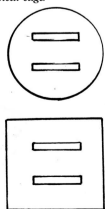

Runners or cleats are glued or tacked in position on under-side of base boards.

For square or rectangular base boards, trim corners of excess paper and glue down margin.

For round or curved base boards, the margin of the paper is slashed with scissors at 1.5-cm (¾-in) intervals to make a neat edge when folded over and glued.

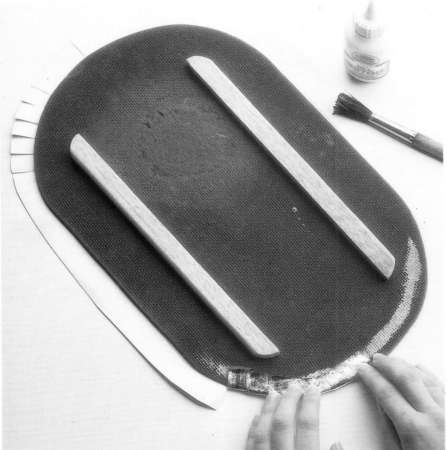

SIMPLE TECHNIQUES
COVERING THE CAKE

Step 1
Pack small pieces of marzipan or almond paste into any holes in cake.

Step 2
Brush cake with lightly beaten egg white or purée of apricot jam.

Step 3
Use rolling pin to lift rolled-out marzipan or almond paste on to cake.

Step 4
Knead sugar paste before rolling out applying to cake in the same way as the marzipan or almond paste.

The covering of a cake is an important step in ensuring a perfectly finished cake. As all good decorators know, no matter how much skill is applied in design and ornamentation, an uneven base will detract from the overall appearance of a completed cake. So obtaining a smooth, flaw-free surface is a vital first step.

Preparation of cake prior to covering

After the cake is cooked, remove from the oven immediately and wrap in an old blanket or towels for 24 hours as the cake cools. When cold, remove from the tin (pan) and carefully peel away the paper lining. Take great care on the corners as these can be easily broken. Any unevenness on the top surface needs to be trimmed away so that the cake is absolutely level and the sides are all the same height. Most decorators turn the cake upside down before covering as the base is always perfectly flat and the top is not. Before proceeding further, place the cake on a piece of greaseproof (wax) paper.

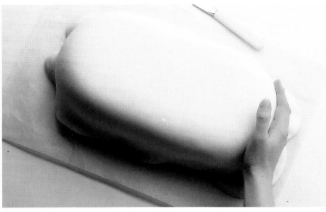

Step 5
After smoothing the top, press the icing on the sides to attach it securely.

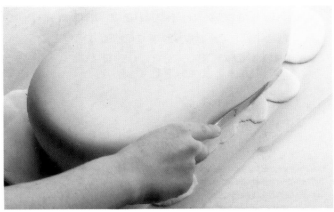

Step 6
Cut away excess icing.

Step 7
Trim the greaseproof (wax) paper to edge of cake.

Step 8
Place cake on prepared base board.

Packing with marzipan or almond paste

Fruit holes, paper creases, cavities or uneven corners need to be filled in or 'packed' with marzipan or almond paste. Use a small blade table knife for packing pieces of paste into the empty spaces. Press well with the blade of the knife to ensure the packing is level with the surface of the cake. Brush the cake lightly all over with egg white or the purée of apricot jam. Take care not to apply too much as this may cause seepage later.

Covering with marzipan or almond paste

Knead the marzipan or almond paste very well. Sprinkle the work surface with sifted icing (confectioner's) sugar and roll the paste to the size that will cover the complete area of the cake. Be sure to roll to an even thickness. Using a rolling pin, lift the paste and transfer it to the cake. Smooth the paste on with the palms of the hands. Start at the top, and then press down the sides. Cake smoothers from cake decorating suppliers may be a help.

Trim the excess paste away from the base by holding the knife at right angles to the side of the cake and cutting cleanly.

Cakes covered with almond paste need to stand for 2 days before the next covering to allow the almonds to dry. A cake covered with marzipan needs 12 hours' drying time.

Covering the cake with sugar paste

Brush the surface of the cake very lightly with egg white or purée of apricot jam. Knead the sugar paste (fondant) until smooth and pliable. Dust the work surface lightly with cornflour (cornstarch) or icing sugar and roll out the icing evenly to a size to cover the cake. Use a tape measure to check size. If any air bubbles appear in the surface of the icing, prick these with a fine needle or a pin to release the trapped air. Do not roll the icing too thinly as this will result in a poor cover and will show any lumps from the first coat underneath.

Use the rolling pin to raise the icing and lift it on to the cake. Lightly dust your hands with cornflour and rub the top of the cake before adhering the sides. Trim away the excess icing. Do not overdo the rubbing or the icing could become thin along the top edges and corners. Trim the greaseproof paper back level with the cake and with a broad-bladed knife, lift the cake on to the prepared board.

PIPING A NAME

Using a No 00 tube and soft-peak royal icing, pipe the word 'Mother'.

ALPHABET FOR PIPING

When piping words on to a cake, there are no hard and fast rules about the sort of lettering you should use. Many decorators pipe freehand, using a piece of foam to rest their hand on, and to provide a straight bottom edge for their work.

If you are unsure of your ability to pipe letters freehand, trace the words you want from this alphabet on to greaseproof (wax) paper and use it as a stencil.

A B C D E F G H I J K L M

N O P Q R S T U V W X Y Z

a b c d e f g h i j k l m

n o p q r s t u v w x y z

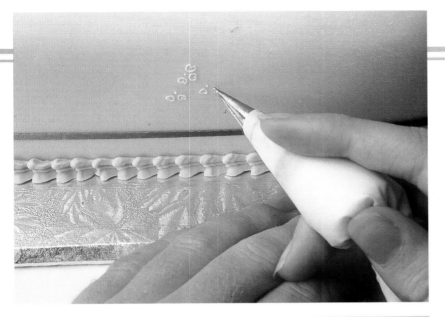

EMBROIDERING THE SIDES

Using a template, mark the main points of the side design on to the cake with a stylus or pin. With a No 00 tube and soft-peak royal icing, embroider the design on to the cake.

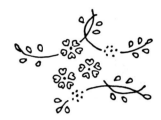

BASIC EMBROIDERY FOR THE BEGINNER

Basic embroidery

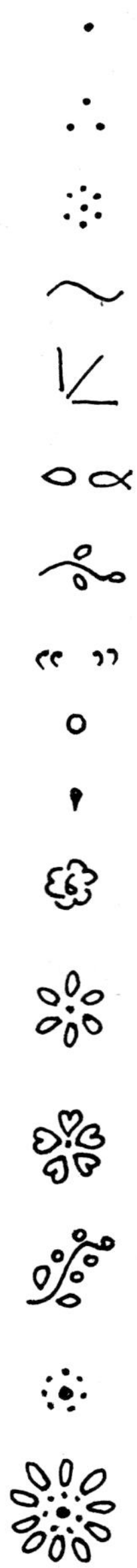

- Dot
- Three dots
- Forget-me-nots
- Curved line
- Straight lines
- Leaf (two varieties)
- Curved line and leaf
- Apostrophes
- Hollyhock
- Teardrop
- Rose
- Daisy
- Primula
- Curved line and small circles
- Large dot and smaller dots
- Flower with dots in centre

- Hollyhock
- Three dots
- Leaf
- Dot

- Primula
- Curved line
- Apostrophes

Examples of simple embroidery patterns

- Dot
- Three dots
- Curved line
- Leaf
- Apostrophes
- Daisy

- Straight line
- Teardrop
- Dot

- Large dot
- Three dots
- Leaf
- Curved leaf
- Flower with dots

- Hollyhock
- Leaf
- Dot

STEP-BY-STEP BASIC EMBROIDERY

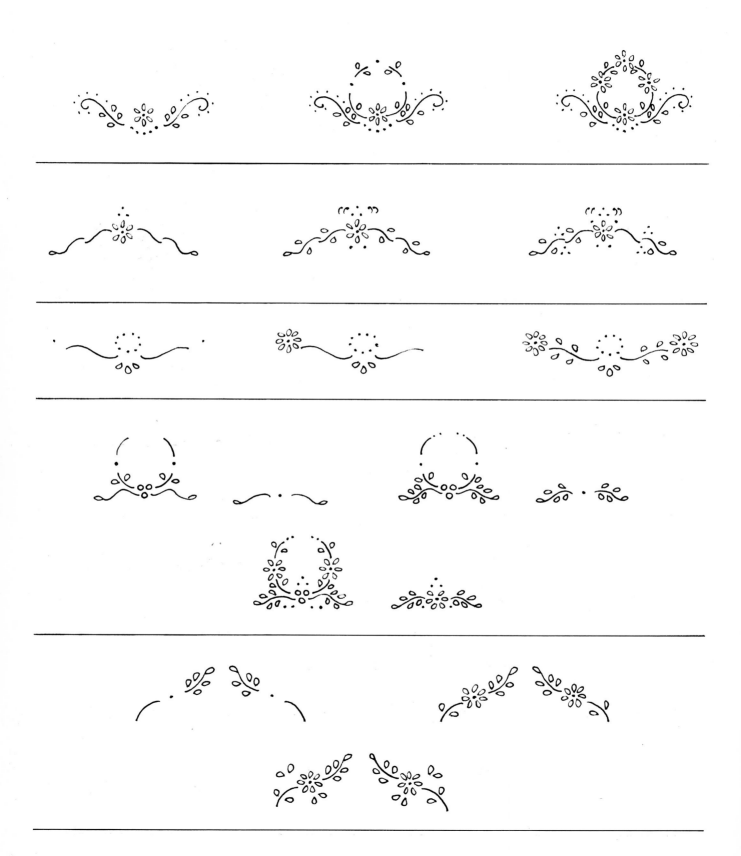

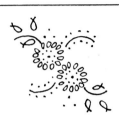

BORDER DESIGNS

EYELET EMBROIDERY

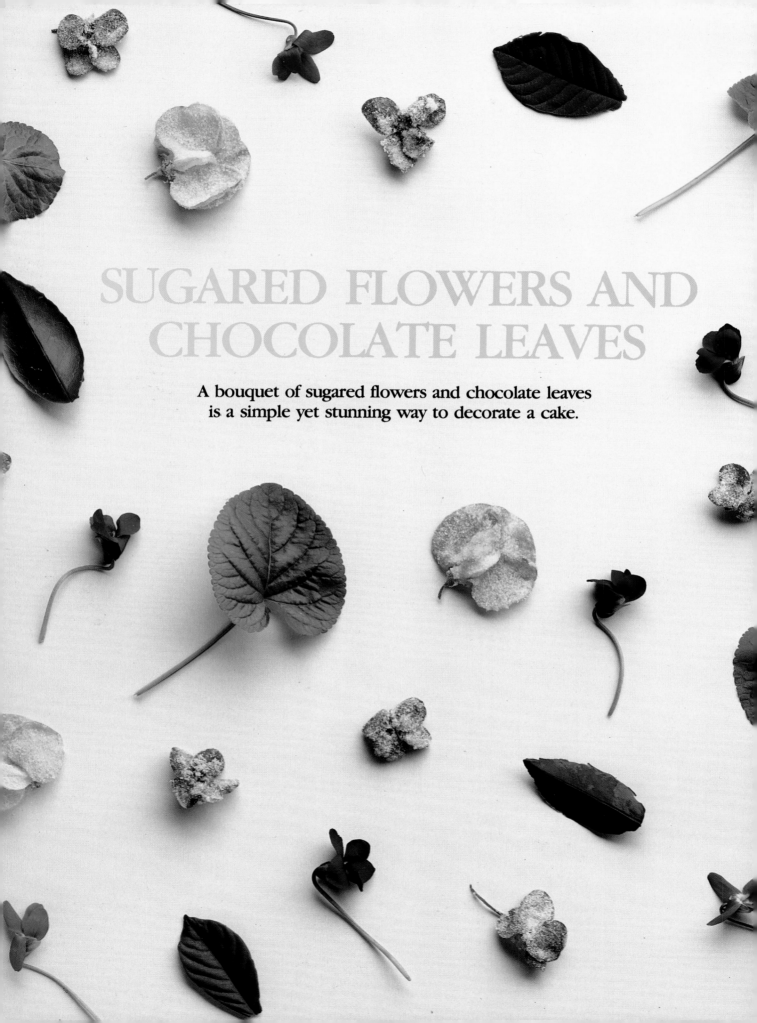

SUGARED FLOWERS AND CHOCOLATE LEAVES

A bouquet of sugared flowers and chocolate leaves
is a simple yet stunning way to decorate a cake.

SUGARED FLOWERS

Choose only flowers that are edible such as violets, roses, sweet peas or nasturtiums. Wash and gently dry with absorbent kitchen paper.

Step 1

Beat an egg white lightly until just mixed without any froth. Use a fine brush to paint a light coating of egg white on both sides of the petals.

Step 2

As each flower is coated, sprinkle with a thick layer of caster sugar. Shake gently to remove any loose sugar. Place the sugared flowers on a fine wire rack and leave to dry for several hours. They can also be dried on a baking sheet in a very slow oven for 8 minutes. Remove immediately and cool.

Step 3

Place sugared flowers on a plate ready to use.

CHOCOLATE LEAVES

Choose firm rigid non-poisonous leaves such as rose or camellia. Wash and dry thoroughly.

Step 1
Melt chopped plain (semisweet) chocolate over hot water.

Step 2
Use a small brush to coat the top side of the leaves thickly with the chocolate.

Step 3
When the chocolate is completely set, hold the stem and peel the real leaf away from the chocolate one.

Note
Ivy leaves look very decorative but great care must be taken not to use a poisonous variety. It is also essential to remove every particle of dust from the veins of each leaf.

SPECIAL OCCASION CAKE
THE WEDDING

This beautiful two-tiered wedding cake is decorated with a Garrett frill and simple embroidery, including eyelets. The moulded flowers are jasmine, forget-me-nots and briar roses.

The cakes in the photograph were baked in octagonal tins, but square or round tins could also be used. When making a tiered cake, make sure that each tier is made in a tin of similar shape and that the height of the bottom tin is greater than the top tin. Here are recommended sizes for tiered cakes:

Two tiers:

30 × 15 cm (12 × 6 in)
25 × 15 cm (10 × 6 in)

Three tiers:

30 × 23 × 15 cm (12 × 9 × 6 in)
25 × 20 × 15 cm (10 × 8 × 6 in)
23 × 18 × 13 cm (9 × 7 × 5 in)

To judge how much marzipan or sugarpaste (fondant) is required to cover a cake, weigh the fruit cake and halve the weight. For example, a 5 kg (10 lb) cake will require 2.5 kg (5 lb) sugarpaste or marzipan.

To prepare a cake before icing

1. Cut a piece of masonite the same shape as the cake. Do not use cardboard, as it will not take the weight of the cake.

2. Cut out a piece of silver or gold paper 1 cm (½ in) larger than the board. Apply paste or wood glue to the board, spread it out evenly and cover the board with the paper. Use a damp tea (dish) towel to smooth out any air bubbles. Put a little more glue on the sides of the board and, using a damp tea towel, pull the paper firmly against the sides and fold over on to the back of the board. Cut another piece of paper, a little smaller than the first piece and glue it to the back.

3. Attach two wooden runners to the base of the board to make the cake easier to pick up. If the board is for the top or second tier of a tiered cake, there is no need for runners.

4. If the cake is not even, cut off the top and place the cake face-down on a plastic place mat. You will now have a level surface to work on.

5. Fill any crease marks, gaps or holes with sugarpaste or marzipan. Roll out a small 'sausage' of sugarpaste and fill in the base of the cake, making sure that the sugarpaste is kept in alignment with the sides of the cake. Press firmly against the cake with a spatula or flat knife so that no ridges or bumps show. Neaten off any excess sugarpaste or marzipan with a sharp knife. Clean off any excess cake crumbs.

6. Before covering the cake with sugarpaste or marzipan, use a pastry brush to apply egg white or boiled and strained jam to the surface of the cake. Use it sparingly. If marzipan is to be applied before the sugarpaste, leave the marzipan for several days to allow it to dry out.

To cover a cake

1. Knead the sugarpaste with a little sifted icing (confectioner's) sugar.

2. Using a clean work surface, roll out the sugarpaste with a rolling pin, putting a little cornflour (cornstarch) under the sugarpaste while rolling it out to prevent it from sticking to the surface. When the sugarpaste is about 1 cm (½ in) thick and approximately the size of the cake, place it on the cake. Do not make it so big that excessive amounts hang over the sides, as its weight when attached will cause hairline cracks to form.

3. After checking that the sugarpaste is the right size, remove it from the cake and brush the cake with boiled sieved jam or egg white.

4. Pick up the sugarpaste on a rolling pin and place it gently on to the cake. Sprinkle a little sifted icing sugar on your hands and smooth the top of the cake with the palm of the hand to eliminate air bubbles, then secure the sugarpaste to the sides.

5. Rub the palm of your hand backwards and forwards against the top edge of the cake to attach the sugarpaste securely to the cake. Press the sugarpaste firmly against the base of the cake before cutting off any excess sugarpaste with a clean sharp knife. Use a wooden plane or a piece of cleaned X-ray film to smooth the sides and top of the cake. (If hairline cracks appear on the top of the cake, quickly cut off the excess sugarpaste and bring the X-ray film up the sides of the cake instead of down as usual; this should eliminate a lot of the cracks.) Prick any air bubbles.

6. If the weather is windy, it is advisable to wait until the wind dies down before icing, or the cake may dry out too quickly.

7. Bring the place mat on which the cake is resting over to the side of the work surface and release each side by pulling the mat downwards. Place your hand under the cake, and after attaching a small piece of royal icing to the board, secure the cake in the centre.

8. If the cake is very large or is an irregular shape, it is easier to ice it straight on to the board, with a piece of waxed paper attached with egg white to the board to keep it clean. This can be cut away when the cake is complete.

JASMINE

Step 1

Dust a small amount of cornflour (cornstarch) on to your fingers. Take a small piece of modelling paste and mould it into the shape of a small funnel. Using a cocktail stick (toothpick), hollow out a cone and cut this into 5 equal parts with scissors.

Step 2

Press each portion firmly between the finger and thumb to thin out the petal to the required thickness. Using a pair of curved nail scissors cut two-thirds down from the centre of the petal until all the petals have been formed.

Step 3

Using a ball tool and a stroking action, thin the petal out from the centre to the edge. Twist some of the petals so that when completed they will not appear flat.

Step 4

Dip a hooked wire into egg white and then insert it through the centre of the jasmine and secure it firmly using a pair of long tweezers. Place a small pale green stamen in the centre of the jasmine. Using leaf-green food colouring, paint a small calyx at the base of the flower. When this is dry, dust or paint with rose pink dusting powder or food colouring the base of the trumpet, leaving the underneath petals white.

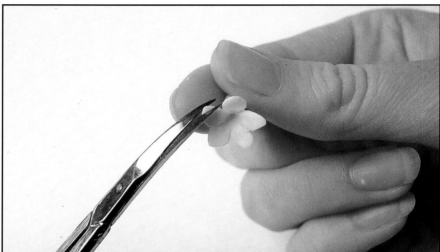

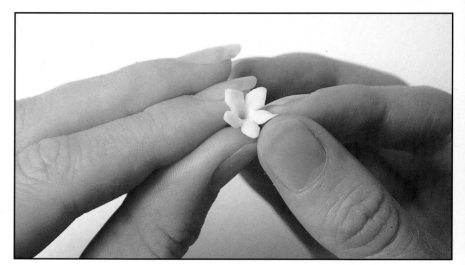

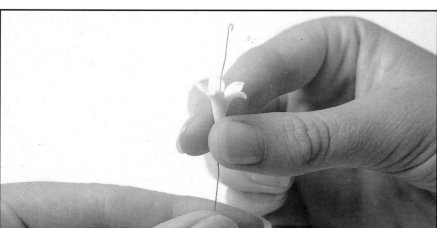

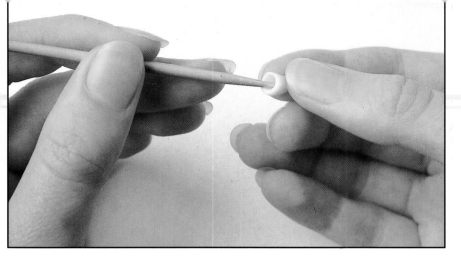

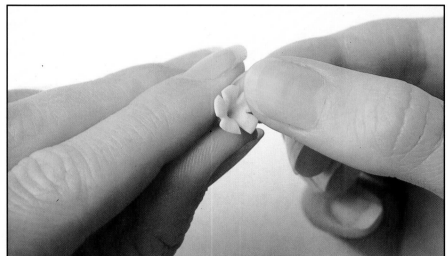

FORGET-ME-NOT

Step 1

Dust a little cornflour (cornstarch) on to your finger-tips. Take a small piece of white modelling paste and mould it into a cone. Using a fine cable knitting needle or cocktail stick (toothpick) hollow out the centre. Using a fine pair of pointed scissors, make 5 equal cuts.

Step 2

Dust a little cornflour on to your finger-tips and gently lift each petal out, to form a circle. Then press the first petal between the finger and thumb and gently squeeze the two sides towards the centre until the petal takes on a rounded shape. Continue in this manner until the five petals have been shaped.

Step 3

Using a large ball tool and a stroking action, thin the petal out from the centre to the edge. Continue until the five petals have been completed. Dip a hooked wire into egg white and insert it firmly into the centre of the flower.

Step 4

Paint the centre of the flower with lemon food colouring using a fine paintbrush. When dry, dust the rest of the flower with a soft blue/mauve dusting powder (non-toxic) mixed with a little cornflour.

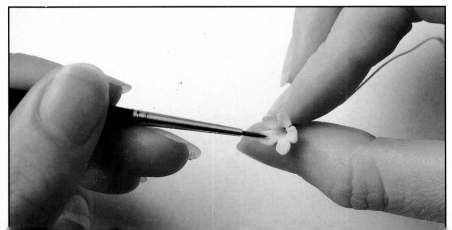

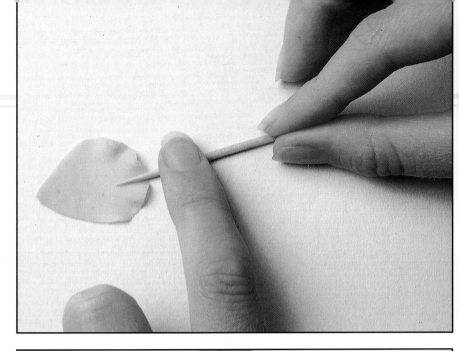

BRIAR ROSE

Step 1

Colour a small piece of modelling paste lightly with liquid rose-pink food colouring. Sprinkle a board lightly with cornflour (cornstarch) and using a small rolling pin, roll out the modelling paste thinly. Cut out five petals using a large rose cutter. Put four of these in an airtight container. Put the remaining petal on a laminated surface, lightly dusted with cornflour. Dip the index finger or thumb into a mixture of soft pink dusting powder and cornflour and colour the top of the petal. Using a cocktail stick (toothpick), roll back and forwards, fluting around the top edge of the petal and thinning it out at the same time.

Step 2

Dust your hands with cornflour and place the petal in the palm of your hand. Press the top three-quarters of the petal lightly and at the same time squeeze the thumb towards the centre of your hand to curve the petal. Cut out another 5 small rose petals and shape these in the same manner as the large petals.

Step 3

Lay a square of foil over a large macrame ring and press it into the shape of the of the ring. Using a No 5 star tube, pipe a large dot of lemon-coloured royal icing into the centre of the foil. Place each of the large outside petals in the royal icing, slightly overlapping the petals. The smaller inside petals are placed, shaded side up, inside the larger petals, using a little more royal icing to attach them. They should slightly overlap each other. Tuck the last petal in at an angle.

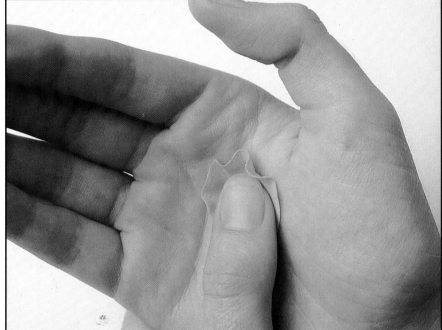

Step 4
Cut lemon-coloured stamens to various lengths and curve them over your finger. With a No 5 star tube squeeze out another dot of firm-consistency lemon-coloured royal icing in the centre of the flower. Place the stamens in position using long tweezers.

ROSEBUDS

Step 1
Using a medium-sized rose cutter, cut and mould three rose petals using the same method as given in step 1 of Briar Rose.

Step 2
Put firm-peak royal icing in an icing bag and using a No 5 tube, pipe a star in the centre of a square of waxed paper.

Step 3
Place the three dried petals in the centre of the royal icing in the shape of a triangle.

Step 4
Then pull the waxed paper up firmly around the petals. Give the paper a slight twist and leave to dry. When dry, remove the paper.

Step 5
Make a three-pointed calyx from leaf green-coloured modelling paste and attach it with egg white to the bud.

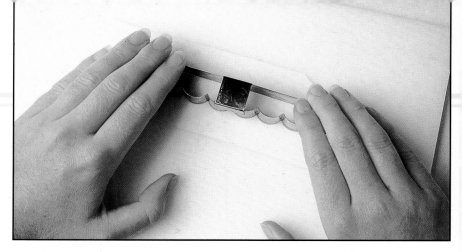

GARRETT FRILL

This frill was devised by the well-known South African decorator, Elaine Garrett.

Step 1

Knead a little sugar into a piece of fondant until the fondant is quite firm but not sticky. Sprinkle a little cornflour (cornstarch) on to a board and roll out the fondant thinly. Using a Garrett frill cutter, cut out the frill and place it on a laminated surface which has been dusted with cornflour.

Step 2

Press a wooden cocktail stick (toothpick) into the base of the fondant shape. Roll it backwards and forwards to form a frill, continuing in this manner until the whole piece has been completed.

Step 3

Tuck the left-hand side of the frill under, using a paintbrush dipped in egg white to attach the frill to the cake. Using a small piece of plastic wrap, gently rub the top of the frill against the surface of the cake to eliminate any joins. Continue in this manner until the base of the cake is surrounded with the frill. Lift the frill up with a cocktail stick to soften the flounce.

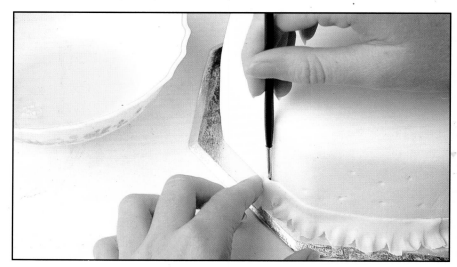

Step 4

Make small posies of forget-me-nots, jasmine and leaves and attach one to each corner of the cake with a small hairpin of wire, covered with green plastic floristry tape. Use tweezers to do this.

Note

Sugar flowers attached in this way must only be used for display purposes. Great care should always be taken to ensure that there is no possibility of any wire particles being eaten accidentally.

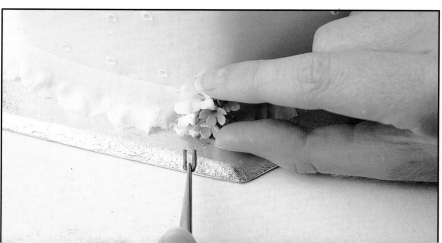

EMBROIDERY

Step 1
Make a template from greaseproof (wax) paper, approximately half the height of the cake and the length of one of the sides. Draw the design on to the greaseproof template in pencil. Using a pin, prick out the main points, e.g. eyelet work and centre of flowers.

Step 2
Make soft-peak royal icing. Using a fine cable needle, mark out the eyelet work. With royal icing and a No 00 writing tube, embroider the three holes, piping in a circular fashion on top of the holes.

Step 3
Pipe the centre of the flowers using a large dot for the centre and smaller dots around it to form a circle. Continue until all the centres have been piped.

Step 4
Still using a No 00 writing tube and soft-peak royal icing, pipe the outside petals of the flowers, curved lines and leaves. Continue this process until all the sides of the cake have been embroidered.

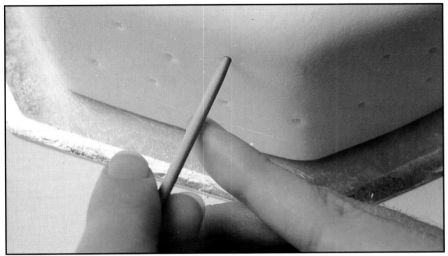

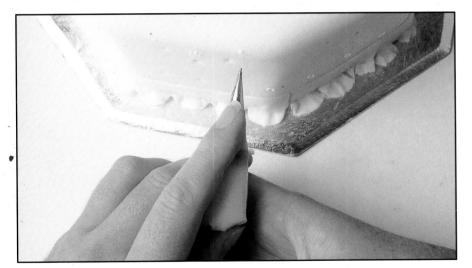

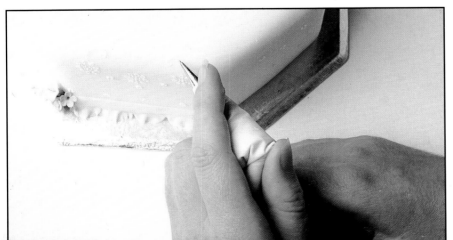

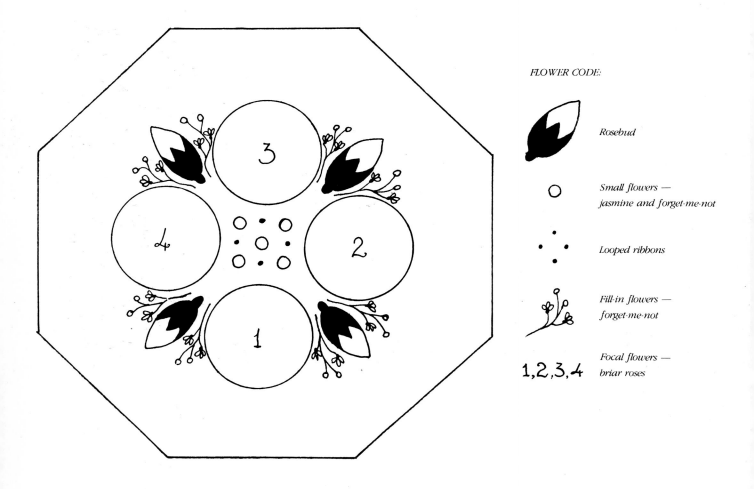

FLOWER CODE:

Rosebud

Small flowers —
jasmine and forget-me-not

Looped ribbons

Fill-in flowers —
forget-me-not

1,2,3,4   Focal flowers —
briar roses

To arrange flowers on the top tier of the cake

1. Make four holes in the centre of the cake (approximately 1.75 cm (¾ in) apart) using a long pair of tweezers.

2. With the aid of the tweezers, push the looped ribbons into the cake in an upright position.

3. Place flowers in position at an angle, *not flat*, resting them against the looped ribbon. Secure briar rose No 1 (see diagram) with a dab of royal icing underneath the petal.

4. Place the other roses (Nos 2, 3 and 4) on a piece of thin foam and mark where each will sit on the cake before continuing.

5. Squeeze a small amount of royal icing under the rosebuds and place them between Nos 1 and 2, and 1 and 4.

6. Make a hole with a pair of tweezers either side of the buds and insert a spray of flowers into each hole. Neaten up the gaps with royal icing and a damp paintbrush.

7. Attach No 2 by placing a small amount of royal icing under the petal. Rest the flower against the looped ribbon.

8. Place the next rosebud between Nos 2 and 3, making a hole either side of the bud and inserting the small sprays. Again neaten up the gaps with royal icing.

9. With a pair of long-pointed tweezers, arrange the single flowers in the centre of the cake neatening up the holes with royal icing and making sure the flowers are at different heights and only just above the main flowers.

10. Complete the arrangement by placing Nos 3 and 4 in position, using the same method as before, then squeeze royal icing

under the petals and join the flowers either side of the rosebuds.

The same technique is used to decorate the bottom tier. See the photograph on page 33 for the flower arrangement.

Important points to remember

1. Make sure the flowers are centred correctly, otherwise the whole arrangement will be unbalanced and unsymmetrical.

2. Position the buds so that they are not in alignment with the focal flowers.

3. When inserting the small sprays of flowers into the cake, place them so that they form a different line from the buds or focal flowers.

4. If the completed arrangement is successful, it will form a circle when viewed from above.

5. Never place this arrangement flat on a cake – always elevate the flowers.

To place pillars on a tiered cake

You will need

wooden meat skewers
pillars
greaseproof (wax) paper template of top tier
base board

Method

1. Make a greaseproof paper template of the base board for the top tier. Fold it in half, then in half again. Push a skewer through the four pieces of paper (see diagram).

2. Put the template in the centre of the bottom tier. Position the pillars on the paper.

3. Insert the wooden skewers into the cake, then pull them back out and turn them over so that the point is facing upwards.

4. Replace the skewers in the cake and this time, using a pen, mark the skewers just above the point where the top of the pillar reaches. Remove them from the cake.

5. Cut off the skewers at the places marked. Remove the greaseproof template and insert the skewers back through the pillars and into the cakes.

6. When this process is completed, the weight of the cake should be on the wooden skewers – not on the pillars, which are normally of a fairly flimsy construction.

Greaseproof template

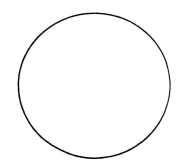

Greaseproof paper template of the base board for the top tier

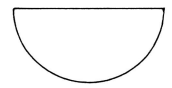

Template folded in half

Folded in half again. Mark where the skewers will sit on the cake

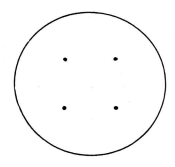

Push the skewers into the cake

To cut a wedding cake

The first cut, or ceremonial cut, should be from the centre of the cake to the edge and then down to the board. The cake is then usually removed to the kitchen where it is cut into pieces for the guests. Use an extremely sharp knife with a 25–30-cm (10–12-in) blade. Never attempt to cut wedges, cut the cake in half, and then into slices. Cut each slice into pieces, according to how many guests you are serving.

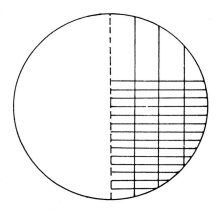

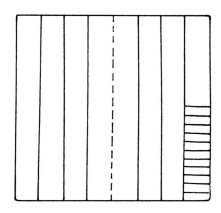

To keep the top tier of a wedding cake

The best way to do this is to put it in an airtight plastic container and freeze it. Defrost it with the lid on, and even after 12 months, it will be in good condition.

This enchanting cake will delight any new baby's
family and friends at the gathering after that very
important occasion in a baby's life – the Christening.

This cake is suitable for the christening of either a baby boy or a girl. The base board was covered with sugarpaste (fondant) and edged with a trim of thin foil ribbon. The cake has a base cover of almond paste which was allowed to dry for 2 days before the top cover of sugarpaste was applied. After the sugarpaste firmed the Garrett frills were added. The novelties and tiny blossoms were made from modelling paste. A little royal icing was used to attach them to the cake. Royal icing was also used for the embroidery and the leaves.

Christening Cake

250 g (8 oz, 1½ cups) sultanas (golden raisins)
250 g (8 oz, 1½ cups) raisins
125 g (4 oz, 1⅔ cups) currants
125 g (4 oz, ¾ cup) glacé (candied) cherries, chopped
125 g (4 oz, ¾ cup) mixed peel
125 g (4 oz, ¾ cup) glacé fruit, chopped
125 ml (4 fl oz, ½ cup) brandy
250 g (8 oz, 1 cup) butter
250 g (8 oz, 1½ cups) brown sugar
grated rind of 1 lemon
30 ml (2 tbsp) orange marmalade
4 eggs, beaten
280 g (9 oz, 2¼ cups) plain (all-purpose) flour, sifted
large pinch of nutmeg
large pinch of cinnamon
2.5 ml (½ tsp) mixed spice

Put all the fruits in a bowl and pour on the brandy. Leave to soak for at least 24 hours. Cream the butter and sugar until light and fluffy. Add the lemon rind and marmalade and beat in the eggs gradually. Add the fruit alternately with the flour and spices. Spoon the mixture into a lined 20-cm (8-in) oval tin (pan) and bake at 140°C (275°F, Gas 1) for 3–3½ hours or until a thin skewer comes out clean when inserted into cake. Wrap cake while still hot in several towels and allow to cool in the tin.

Almond Paste

750 g (1½ lb, 4½ cups) icing (confectioner's) sugar, sifted
250 g (8 oz, 2¼ cups) ground almonds
3 egg yolks
30 ml (2 tbsp) brandy or sherry
15 ml (1 tbsp) lemon juice

Mix together the sifted icing sugar and ground almonds in a large bowl. Beat together the egg yolks, brandy and lemon juice. Make a well in the centre of the icing sugar and ground almonds and add the liquid gradually to make a firm paste. Sprinkle work surface with sifted icing sugar and knead the almond paste well. If the paste is too dry, add a little extra lemon juice. If the paste is too moist, mix in a little sifted icing sugar. Almond paste can be used immediately.

Sugarpaste

(to cover a 20-cm (8-in) cake)
60 ml (2 fl oz, ¼ cup) water
25 ml (5 tsp) powdered gelatine
125 ml (4 fl oz, ½ cup) liquid glucose
23 ml glycerine, measured in a medicine glass
1 kg (2 lb, 6 cups) icing (confectioner's) sugar, sifted into a bowl
flavouring essence

Put the water in a very small saucepan and sprinkle on the gelatine. Heat gently, stirring constantly until the gelatine is dissolved. Do not use too much heat and do not boil. Remove from heat and mix in glucose and glycerine. Add to the sifted icing sugar and mix with hands to a firm dough. Add flavouring essence. Turn on to a surface lightly dusted with cornflour (cornstarch) and knead well until smooth and pliable.

If the icing is too soft, add extra icing sugar. If it is too firm, add a little hot water. Place icing in a plastic bag and then in an airtight plastic container until ready to use. The icing may be used within 1 hour of making or it will keep indefinitely.

Royal Icing

1 egg white, at room temperature approximately
250 g (8 oz, 1½ cups) icing (confectioner's) sugar, sifted three times
1 drop of acetic acid

Follow the instructions on page 85 for making Royal icing. Colour and use as required for the cake.

Use white icing to attach the novelties and tiny blossoms. For the *alphabet boxes*, join up the squares of modelling paste with white icing, and neaten the edges with a small shell tube and white icing. Pipe the leaves with green icing and a small leaf pipe; use blue icing and a fine writing pipe for the embroidery. Make the alphabet letters described on page 47 with pink icing.

Modelling Paste

25 ml (5 tsp) water
7.5 ml (1½ tsp) powdered gelatine
10 ml (2 tsp) liquid glucose
250 g (8 oz, 1½ cups) icing (confectioner's) sugar, sifted

Put the water in a very small saucepan and sprinkle on the gelatine. Heat gently, stirring constantly until gelatine is dissolved. Do not use too much heat and do not boil. Remove from heat and add liquid glucose. Mix well. Put the icing sugar in a bowl and mix in the gelatine mixture. Knead well until the mixture is a smooth pliable paste. Place in a plastic bag and put into a sealed container until ready to use.

The correct consistency of the paste is like ready-to-shape plasticine. If the paste is too dry, add a little hot water. If the paste is too soft, add more sifted icing sugar.

THE GARRETT FRILL (make 10)

To make the frill, roll out a piece of sugarpaste thinly and cut out using the Garrett frill cutter. Softly flute the outer edge using a cocktail stick (toothpick) or a similar tool. Roll quickly and firmly along each scallop and lift the frill as you work to encourage more flounce. It is easier to work on a half circle at a time. Moisten the back of the first scallop with water and attach this to the cake. Fold either end of the frill under about 5mm (¼ in) and carefully overlap the left-hand edge as each section is applied. Make sure the joins of each scallop are not obvious but look as if they were one continuous frill around the entire cake. When the last scallop is attached, raise the right-hand side of the first scallop and slip the last one slightly under.

Roll out the sugarpaste and cut with the Garrett frill cutter.

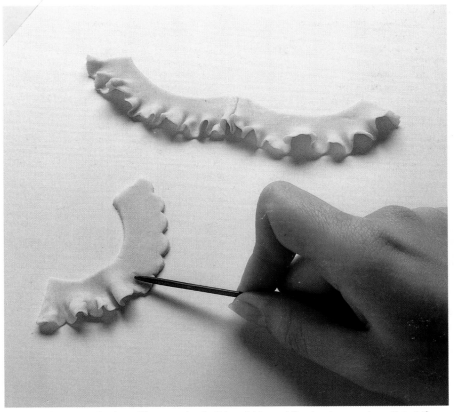

Flute the outer edge by rolling a cocktail stick quickly and firmly along each scallop. Lift as you work to encourage more flounce.

THE FLOWERS
(make about 45)

Roll out modelling paste. Use a small blossom cutter to stamp out flowers. Lift flowers on to thick sponge foam and shape into flowers by firmly pressing a small ball tool into each. Colour with either liquid or powder colouring.

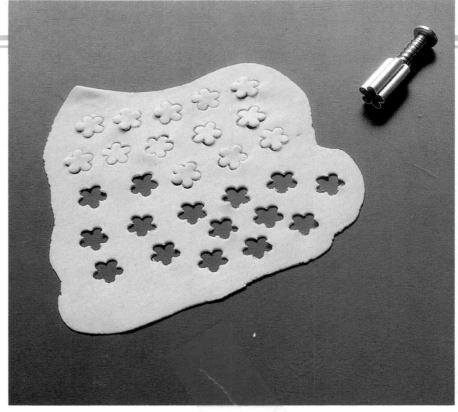

Roll out modelling paste and cut with small blossom cutter for flowers.

Place cut-out blossom shapes on a thick piece of plastic foam and press down with a ball tool. When dry colour with powder or liquid colourings.

THE ALPHABET BOXES (make 2)

Roll out modelling paste and cut twelve 4-cm (1½-in) squares. Allow each piece to dry flat, turning at regular intervals to dry both sides. When hard, join the pieces together with firm royal icing to form a cube. Neaten edges by piping a small shell border. When royal icing is dry, attach alphabet letters with a dab of royal icing.

Join dried squares of modelling paste together with firm royal icing.

Use a small shell tube and white royal icing to finish the alphabet boxes.

The Alphabet Letters

These may be piped directly on to the finished box. Another way is to write letters with pencil on paper, cover with greaseproof (wax) paper and pipe icing over the letters. Allow to dry before removing.

Pipe letters for the alphabet boxes on greaseproof paper placed over printed letters. Allow to dry before removing.

THE TEDDY BEAR

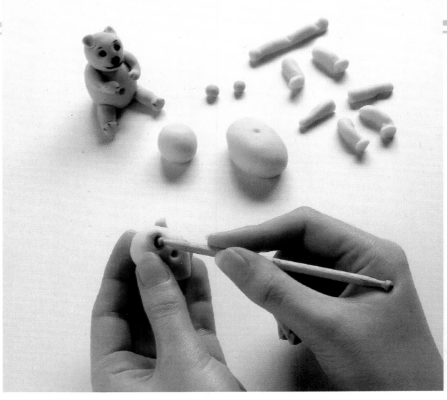

Head

Mix equal quantities of modelling paste and sugarpaste and colour caramel brown. Take a small piece and roll it in the palms of the hands into a round ball. Elongate to form the nose. Cut the mouth with a scalpel and open a little. Roll two small pea-sized balls for the ears and then position on each side of the head with a small ball tool. Use the same tool to indent the eyes.

Body

Shape a ball of modelling paste in proportion to the size of the head into an oval.

Legs

Roll a sausage-shaped piece of modelling paste to the thickness required and cut it into two identical lengths. Shape slightly into the ankle and press the foot to flatten the sole.

Arms

Roll a sausage-shaped length as described for the legs, shape into the wrist and flatten the paw slightly.

Allow all the pieces to dry thoroughly before assembling.

To assemble

Attach the head, arms and legs to the body with firm royal icing. Allow to dry. Pipe in the eyes with brown royal icing. Soften brown royal icing with a little egg white and pipe over the body, arms and legs for the fur. Roughen icing with the end of the piping tube. Paint in details such as claws, mouth and eyebrows and insert a small piece of red modelling paste in the open mouth for the tongue. Use a thin strip of red paste to make the bow tie.

To make the ears, position pea-sized balls of paste and push into place with a small ball tool.

THE DOLL

Take a small ball of modelling paste for the head. Take another slightly larger piece for the body and taper at one end. Slit the tapered end with a scalpel or scissors to form the legs. Separate slightly and pinch the ends to form the feet.

Roll a piece of modelling paste long enough to form the arms. Flatten at each end for the hands and attach the strip across the top of the body with a little water. Allow all pieces to dry before painting on the face. Attach the head with firm royal icing and pipe a cone hat using a shell tube.

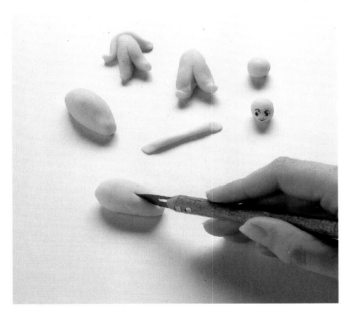

THE RABBIT

Take a small ball of modelling paste for the head. Pinch out the nose, and shape the ears with a small ball tool. Make a ball for the body, then shape into an oval. Roll a small sausage-shaped length and cut two even-sized pieces to form the arms and two slightly longer pieces for the legs. Allow all pieces to dry before assembling with firm royal icing. Pipe on a fluffy tail, paint eyes, mouth and nose.

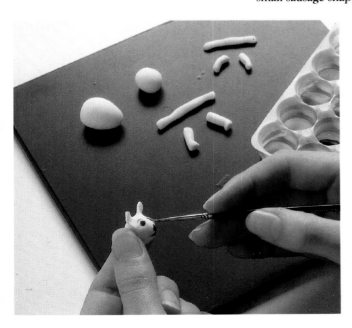

PETITS FOURS

Delicate little morsels that should be only one
mouthful in size, petits fours always surprise and
delight guests.

Petits fours are made from a plain genoise cake and the following recipe will yield about 72 petits fours. The quantities given here for topping and icing are enough to cover one-third of the quantity of genoise.

Genoise (for 72 petits fours)

3 eggs
125 g (4 oz, ½ cup) caster (superfine) sugar
few drops of vanilla essence
60 g (2 oz, ½ cup) plain (all-purpose) flour, sifted
30 g (1 oz, 2 tbsp) butter, melted and cooled

Topping (for 24 petits fours)

155 g (5 oz, ½ cup) apricot jam
15 ml (1 tbsp) water
90 g (3 oz, ⅓ cup) marzipan (see page 8)

Icing (for 24 petits fours)

15 ml (1 tbsp) liquid glucose
45 – 60 ml (3 – 4 tbsp) warm water
345 g (11 oz, 2 cups) icing (confectioner's) sugar, sifted
few drops of food colouring

Step 1

Line a greased 28 × 23-cm (11 × 9-in) cake tin (pan) with greaseproof (wax) or baking paper. Preheat the oven to 180°C (350°F, Gas 4).

Step 2

Combine the eggs and sugar in a medium-sized mixing bowl. Place the bowl in a pan of hot water and beat until the mixture is very thick and just warm. When you lift the beaters the mixture should form a ribbon trail. Remove from the heat and add vanilla essence. Continue beating until mixture is almost cool.

Step 3

Fold in the flour and add the melted butter. Mix well, but do not beat. Pour the mixture into the prepared tin and smooth over the top.

Step 4

Bake for 20–25 minutes or until a skewer inserted into the centre comes out clean. Cool the tin on a wire rack for 10 minutes, then run a knife around the edge of the cake and invert on to a wire rack to cool. Use within 24 hours.

Step 5

To make the topping, push the jam through a fine sieve (strainer) into a small saucepan and stir in the water. Cook over low heat, stirring constantly for 1–2 minutes or until the mixture is smooth. Cool slightly. Cut the cake into thirds if you do not require it all at once. Well wrapped, the genoise will keep for up to 6 weeks in the freezer. Using a pastry brush, brush the topping mixture over the top of the cake.

Step 6

Put the marzipan on a sheet of greaseproof (wax) paper and lay another sheet on top. Roll the marzipan out thinly, remove the top sheet of greaseproof and invert the cake on to the marzipan.

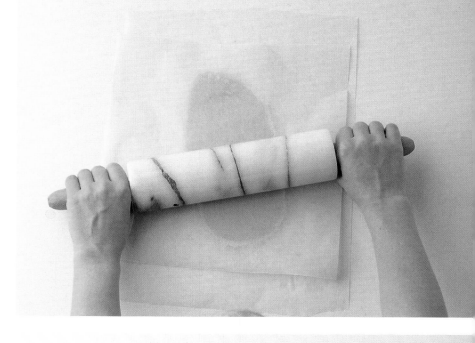

Step 7

Trim the marzipan edges to the size of the cake. Chill for 30 minutes.

Step 8

Using a very sharp knife, cut the cake into 2.5-cm (1-in) squares and chill until firm.

Step 9

To make round petits fours, use a pastry cutter to cut out circles of cake. Brush the top and sides with the topping. Cut out circles of marzipan with the same-sized pastry cutter and place on top of the cakes. Cut strips of marzipan the same width as the height of the cakes and roll the cakes in them to coat the sides.

Step 10

To make the icing, combine glucose and 30 ml (2 tbsp) of water in a bowl set over a pan of simmering water. Add icing sugar and mix well. Add another 15–30 ml (1–2 tbsp) of warm water and continue mixing until smooth. Tint with food colouring – pastel shades are usually used. Place the little cakes on a wire rack and carefully spoon the icing over them. Leave until set.

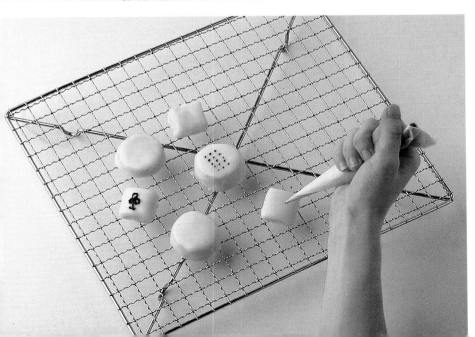

Step 11

Decorate the petits fours with icing, made from icing sugar, water and food colouring, or with melted chocolate. Use a piping bag for the most delicate results. Serve petits fours in paper petits fours cases available from most kitchen equipment shops or stationers.

ADVANCED TECHNIQUES
SWEET PEAS

Follow these steps to make this beautiful spray of sweet peas.

The sweet peas are made from modelling paste (see page 44 for recipe). You will also need a small rose cutter for the bud, a winged sweet pea cutter and an outer petal cutter for the petals, firm floristry wire and powder colourings. The leaves are made with green modelling paste and you will need a leaf cutter, a small calyx cutter, and some green floristry tape.

Step 1

To make a **closed sweet pea bud**, take a length of wire and make a small hook on one end. Insert wire hook into a small cone of modelling paste. Taper both ends and flatten slightly. Then roll more modelling paste to a medium thickness. Use the small rose cutter to cut a petal shape. Moisten one side of the petal with a little water and attach it to the prepared base. Press firmly to make a pod shape. Tilt the top to make a slight curve. Allow paste to firm before the next step.

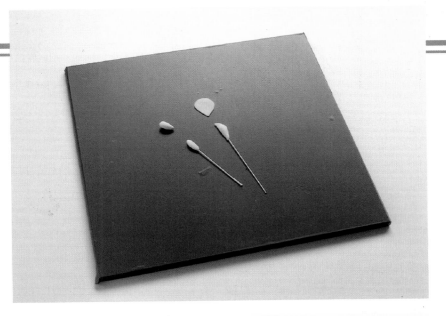

Step 2

To make a **sweet pea bud**, roll the modelling paste out finely. Use the winged sweet pea cutter to cut one petal. Frill the edges using a cocktail stick (toothpick). Moisten the top and sides of the pod and attach the petal from its centre to form two petals, one on each side of the pod.

To make a **fully opened sweet pea**, cut a petal with the outer petal cutter. Frill the edges with a cocktail stick. Place the petal along the index finger and pinch a slight ridge down the centre of the petal. Use a little water to attach the outer petal to the bud with the pinched ridge at the back. Open the flower slightly by holding ridge and very gently easing the outer petal backwards.

Step 3

When the sweet peas are completely dry, brush with dusting powder.

Step 4

Tint paste with green colouring and roll out. Use a small calyx cutter to cut calyx for the base of the sweet pea. To make the leaves, insert wire into small buds of modelling paste. Roll out and cut with a leaf cutter. Mark veins.

Step 5

To soften the leaf edge roll a small ball tool around the edge to produce a soft curl.

Step 6

Stretch, twist and wind green floristry tape around a skewer to make the tendrils.

TO ASSEMBLE THE SWEET PEA SPRAY

To assemble the spray you will also need 15 cm (6 in) strong wire, floristry tape, thin satin ribbon and dried gyposphila (baby's breath).

Attach the buds and the smaller flowers to the strong wire with floristry tape. Then group and attach the fuller flowers to the wire until the spray is the size you want. Place leaves and tendrils so that any gaps are filled in. Hide wires by binding with the thin ribbon. The dried gyposphila is then added to soften the overall effect.

ADVANCED TECHNIQUES
BRUSH FLOODWORK

Completed plaque.

It takes a bit of practice to master the art of floodwork, but when done correctly it creates a beautiful effect.

Brush floodwork is a cake decorating technique, whereby a mural or design is transferred on to a plaque or cake by the use of diluted coloured royal icing and a paintbrush.

A design for brush floodwork

You will need

plaque or cake
HB pencil
tracing paper or greaseproof (wax) paper
non-toxic chalks
liquid food colourings
sable paintbrush No 00 or 000
larger paintbrush (for larger areas)
small laminated board
royal icing
knife
water
small piece of thin foam

After deciding whether to do your work on a plaque or a cake, make sure the surface is quite smooth and completely dry before you start to flood. It is essential not to use too much cornflour (cornstarch) when rolling out your plaque, or it will make the surface hard to flood on.

Method

1. Select a design suitable for the type of cake you are working on, e.g. christening, birthday, or Christmas cake.

2. With an extremely sharp HB pencil, trace the selected drawing on to the greaseproof paper.

3. Turn the tracing over and retrace the sketch on the opposite side, making sure the lead of the pencil does not smudge.

4. Turn the drawing back to the right side, so that the completed drawing is now facing you. Place the greaseproof paper on the plaque or cake and trace the drawing lightly on to the prepared surface.

5. Draw in a light background before starting your brush floodwork. (Take a thin piece of foam to rest your hand on the cake or plaque, to prevent any sweat from your hands getting on to the cake.)

6. Using suitable coloured non-toxic chalks (e.g. green and blue for the grass and sky) and a sable eye make-up brush,

The design has been traced on to the plaque and the background dusted with a sable paintbrush and a mixture of cornflour and grated chalk. Paint in the background of the design first in liquid food colourings. Start flooding the areas farthest away.

dust in a light background. (Leave patches of white if clouds are required.) Thin the chalks down with cornflour.

7. With liquid food colourings and a good firm sable brush, paint in the background. Let your work dry completely before starting floodwork.

8. Tint freshly-made royal icing with food colourings and thin down with water until it will spread without difficulty. Prick any air bubbles with a pin. Draw a line to see if you have the right consistency. Place a small amount of watered-down royal icing on it. If you can see the line, the royal icing is too thin. If the icing will not spread easily, add more water before continuing. Be very sparing with the food colouring

until you have the right shades. If you need a strong colour like red, thin the royal icing down with straight colouring instead of water. Mix a sufficient amount to finish the work, as it can be quite difficult to match colours exactly.

9. At this stage it is necessary to examine the design very carefully and decide which section is the farthest away. Then start flooding. Allow a crust to form before carrying on to the next portion of the work, making sure that you are achieving a three-dimensional effect.

10. Using a fine paintbrush, complete the design by outlining with additional colour (if necessary).

RABBIT AND CHICKEN PLAQUE BRUSH FLOODWORK

Step 1

1. Take a plaque made of modelling paste and transfer the drawn design on to the plaque using an HB drawing pencil.

2. Dust the background with a sable paintbrush and grated chalk (thinned down with cornflour) of a colour such as green or blue.

WORLD OF CAKES
CROQUEMBOUCHE

Croquembouche, made from a pyramid of choux puffs
or profiteroles is the traditional wedding cake of France.

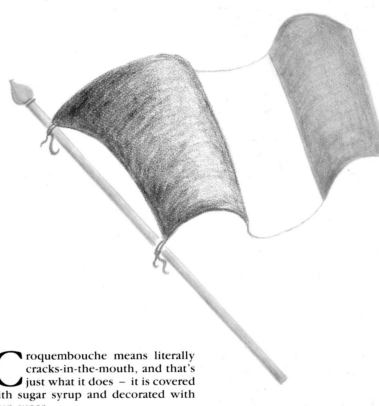

Croquembouche means literally cracks-in-the-mouth, and that's just what it does – it is covered with sugar syrup and decorated with spun sugar.

The history of the croquembouche is fascinating. They were originally phallic symbols, and in France were carried reverently to church in holy processions where they were blessed by the village priests. This custom ended around 1820, but they have remained the traditional wedding cake of France.

A croquembouche is becoming popular with brides in some other countries, especially for summer weddings. It also makes an unusual birthday or celebration cake.

The white sugar flowers that decorate a croquembouche symbolize the bride's virginity, the coloured ones represent children.

Sugared almonds have always been associated with weddings, and today they are often given to guests as a gift from the bride at the weddings of many different cultures. In ancient times almonds were called 'divine fruits' and were thought to have the power to bestow fertility on a couple. Decorating a croquembouche with sugared almonds seems to be a relatively recent custom.

To serve a croquembouche, do not cut with a knife, unless at a wedding and you want to make the first traditional cut. Use a spoon and fork.

The sugar flowers were traditionally white and were a symbol of the bride's virginity. The sugared almonds are a more recent addition to the decorations on the croquembouche. Caramelized sugar syrup is used to join the choux puffs together. The cake is often then covered with strands of spun sugar.

The croquembouche, centrepiece at traditional French wedding receptions.

CASSATA ALLA SICILIANA

Cassata alla Siciliana is one of the great traditional cakes of Sicily.

ALL ABOUT
CHOCOLATE

Cassata alla Siciliana used to be eaten only during the religious festivals of Christmas and Easter and came to signify the beginnings of a new way of life. Now it is served on any day Sicilians want to celebrate.

The cake is part of the sweet-toothed tradition of Sicily that began with the Saracen invasion of the island in the 9th century. The Arabs brought with them a great love for elaborate desserts and the Sicilians soon added their own distinctive touches to create the cakes and desserts for which their island is so famous. For the hard-working Sicilians, industrious by necessity in a land where life can be very hard, Cassata alla Siciliana is more than just a cake. It is a part of the warmth and intensity of the island's festivals. Served as a special treat, its richness and unforgettable taste embody all that is colourful and passionate in Sicily.

For many people, the word cassata brings to mind a type of rich layered ice cream, thick with fruit and nuts. But the traditional cassata is really a variety of cheese cake. There are many, many versions of the cake. Some recipes use sponge fingers to line a mould filled with cream cheese; others specify ice cream between layers of cake. Some cakes are coated with a thick rich frosting; others have a light dusting of icing sugar.

This version is made from a simple butter sponge, baked in a loaf tin. The cake is cut into layers, spread with a liqueur-enriched cream cheese filling and then coated with a rich dark chocolate frosting.

Butter Sponge

125 g (4 oz, ½ cup) butter
185 g (6 oz, ¾ cup) caster (superfine) sugar
grated rind of ½ lemon
2 eggs, lightly beaten
185 g (6 oz, 1½ cups) self-raising flour, sifted
125 ml (4 fl oz, ½ cup) milk

Beat the butter, sugar and the lemon rind until light and fluffy. Add the beaten egg gradually. Mix in a third of the flour and half of the milk. Add another third of the flour and the rest of the milk. Stir in the remaining flour. Pour into a well greased and lined loaf tin and bake at 180°C (350°F, Gas 4) for 50 minutes or until cooked. Leave to stand for 5 minutes before turning on to a wire rack to cool.

Filling

1 kg (2 lb, 4 cups) ricotta or cream cheese
185 g (6 oz, ¾ cup) caster (superfine) sugar
30 ml (2 tbsp) orange-flavoured liqueur
30 ml (2 tbsp) single (light) cream or milk
60 g (2 oz, 2 squares) plain (semisweet) chocolate, finely chopped
125 g (4 oz, ¾ cup) glacé fruit, chopped

Rub the cheese through a coarse wire sieve or blend in a food processor. Beat the cheese, sugar and liqueur together until smooth. Add enough of the cream to make a filling that spreads easily. Fold in the chocolate and the glacé fruit.

Chocolate Frosting

185 ml (6 fl oz, ¾ cup) strong black coffee
750 g (1½ lb) plain (semisweet) chocolate, chopped
250 g (8 oz, 1 cup) unsalted butter, cut into small pieces and chilled

Put the coffee into a small saucepan over a low heat and gradually add the chopped chocolate. Stir until the chocolate melts. Remove from the heat and beat in the butter gradually until the mixture is smooth. Refrigerate until the frosting is firm enough to spread thickly.

To assemble the cake

Trim the top of the cake so that it will sit flat on the serving dish. Cut the cake into three layers horizontally. Join the layers together with the filling. Refrigerate for 2 hours or until the filling is firm. Cover the sides and top of the cake with the chocolate frosting. Fill a piping bag fitted with a star tube and pipe on rosettes and swirls. Top the rosettes with small pieces of glacé fruit. Cover the cake loosely with plastic wrap and refrigerate for 24 hours before serving.

WORKING WITH CHOCOLATE

All chocolate should always be melted without stirring in a double boiler or in a bowl set over hot, but not boiling water. If too hot water is used there is a danger that steam will rise, condense and fall into the melting chocolate and the tiniest drop of water will tighten the chocolate and make it impossible to use. Also, melting chocolate should never be covered with a lid as water can form on the lid and drip into the chocolate.

An emergency treatment for hardened chocolate is to beat in 15–30 ml (1–2 tbsp) soft vegetable fat (shortening). Do not use butter as butter contains a little moisture and it will not solve the problem.

However, it is perfectly all right to add larger quantities of liquid to melting chocolate as this will blend in smoothly. It is just the few drops of liquid that will 'tighten' chocolate. Liquids added can be spirits, coffee, juices or liqueurs. Use at least 15 ml (1 tbsp) of liquid.

Chocolate melts more evenly if it has been chopped or grated first. Chill first before grating on the coarsest grater and use a large knife for chopping chocolate.

Chocolate also melts well in microwave ovens. Spread chocolate on a dish in a single layer and microwave on High for 30 seconds or until chocolate melts.

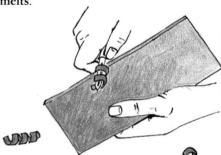

CHOCOLATE CURLS

Chocolate curls are made by letting chocolate stand in a warm place for 15 minutes and then pulling a potato peeler across the surface.

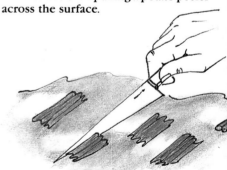

CHOCOLATE SCROLLS

Chocolate scrolls are made by pouring melted warm chocolate on to a cold, flat firm surface and allowing it to set. Pull a large sharp knife held at 45° angle gently through the chocolate to form the scrolls.

EASTER EGGS

An exciting new technique for decorating chocolate Easter eggs imaginatively.

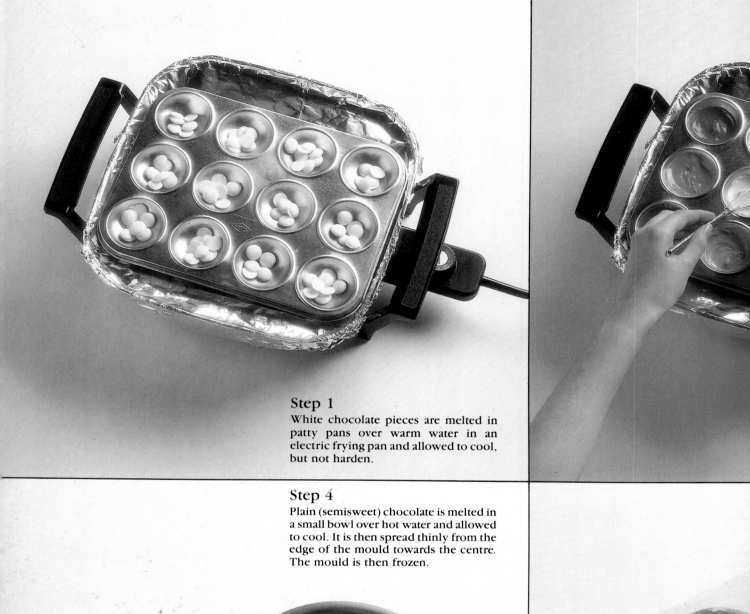

Step 1
White chocolate pieces are melted in patty pans over warm water in an electric frying pan and allowed to cool, but not harden.

Step 4
Plain (semisweet) chocolate is melted in a small bowl over hot water and allowed to cool. It is then spread thinly from the edge of the mould towards the centre. The mould is then frozen.

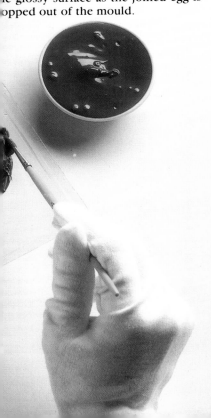

Step 2
...owder colourings are blended in with ...ny whisks. Liquid colourings are not ...sed as they will 'harden' the chocolate.

Step 3
The first layers of colours are painted on the lines of the drawings which have been inked on the outside of the mould. The mould is then frozen until the chocolate is firm. After each colour application, the mould is always frozen or the chocolate lines and layers can melt.

Step 5
...alves are joined by placing one in the ...ould for support and topping with ...nother. The edges are joined by a thick ...yer of chocolate applied with a brush. ...he gloves prevent finger marks spoiling ...e glossy surface as the joined egg is ...pped out of the mould.

Step 6
The finished eggs.

HOW TO WIN A
CAKE DECORATING COMPETITION

It has happened once again. The cake you spent all those long, long hours decorating has not even rated a mention in the judging. You did not really expect to win first prize or even a place, but this time you were sure you had done your best work ever and a Highly Commended card in front of your cake would have been wonderful. The fondant was the smoothest you had ever done; the piping was perfect; you had given a lot of thought to the design and the flowers you had modelled were without a flaw. Family and friends agreed that it was a beautifully decorated cake. You had entered many other cake decorating competitions before and not really been surprised not to rate an award, but this time you were convinced you had created a winner. But after the judging, there was no winning card next to your cake with your name on it. You looked at the cake that was awarded First Prize and you could see it was a little better than yours, but you could not quite see what made it so special and why the judges thought it the best. You begin to wonder where you went wrong and why your entry missed out. You wonder what the judges are looking for when they assess decorated cakes.

In competitive exhibitions a judge

Winning isn't everything but if you would like to do better in cake competitions, it will help if you know what the judges want.

looks for creative ideas, originality, new techniques and the perfection in the execution of such skills by the decorator.

Often judging is broken into specific areas of allocated marks under the following headings:

Presentation
Cake covering and board covering
Suitability of design for its particular class
Visual impact and appeal
Creativity
Difficulty of technique
Execution of design

All **base boards** should be beautifully covered. There is a good choice open to the decorator for covering the board – paper, fabric, royal icing or fondant may be used. But whatever medium is chosen it needs to be neatly and smoothly applied without bumps, wrinkles or tears, unless the design dictates a rough-textured appearance for a novelty section, for example royal icing as snow used as a feature for a Swiss Chalet setting. One point the exhibitor should keep in mind is that the style and texture of the base covering should provide a harmonious complement to the style of the cake itself. The under-side of the base board requires the same care in covering as that given to the top. Cleats

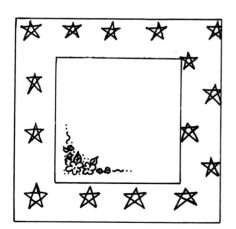

DON'T *choose paper that clashes with the design on cake.*

DO *use paper that complements the cake.*

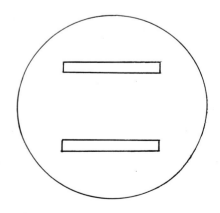

DO *have runners or cleats on the under-side of the base board for support and ease of lifting.*

or runners on the base board may be covered with the same material as used to cover the board, or painted or stained to tone in with the exhibit. Cleats also provide support for the weight of the cake and make it easier to lift.

Base boards should be proportioned to the size of the cake; a small cake looks lost on a too large board, whereas a cake presented on a too small board looks just as absurd. It immediately destroys the balance and visible appeal. The width of the board border is determined by the design; a cake featuring an elaborate extension base will require a slightly larger margin than one with just a plain shell edge.

Base board coverings need to harmonize with the colour scheme of both the cake and its decorations; for example, gold paper should be avoided if using pink tonings, yet it is most suitable with green, cream, yellow and apricot colours. The neutrality of silver is acceptable to most colours.

The **cake covering** should be evenly applied so that no bumps, creases, indentations, specks or dirty smudges are seen. White fondants must be immaculately and crisply white. Coloured fondants need to have the colour evenly dispersed with no tell-tale streaks.

Once covered the cake should be placed on the prepared board to show an even amount of base board all around. Equally, if the design is such that the cake must be set at a particular angle, marks will be lost if the cake is slightly askew.

It is essential that all **pipework** be clearly and well defined. It is here that the skill and control of the decorator is shown, correct pressure assures smooth even piping and providing the royal icing has been well prepared and mixed, it should not have a rough sugary texture.

Correct consistency is necessary for various styles of pipework; for example, shell work requires a firm peak whereas embroidery requires the royal icing to be soft-peak. The firmer icing used for shell work allows the claw marks on each individual shell to be clearly seen. It is wise to balance the size of the shell with that of the cake.

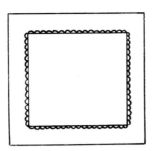

DO *leave adequate border around cake for piping.*

DO *allow for a slightly larger margin with extension work than for piping.*

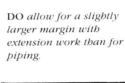

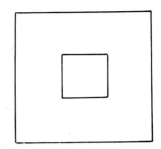

DON'T *place a small cake on too large a board.*

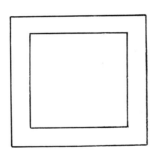

DO *make sure base boards are in proportion to cake size.*

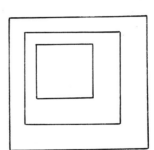

DON'T *place a cake off centre unless the design dictates it (see diagram on left).*

DO *shell work like this.*

DON'T *do shell work like this.*

DO *pipe edges like this.*

DON'T *pipe edges like this.*

Balance is important with tiered cakes; it is essential to grade the cake size as well as the design. If the base covered cake for a three tiered wedding is 8 cm (3½ in) high, then the second tier should be 7.5 cm (3 in) and the top 7 cm (2½ in) in height. Borders, lace and embroidery become slightly smaller also as the tiers increase, yet remain identical as to design. Tiered boards are covered top and completely underneath.

Moulded flowers and leaves should be true to nature. Use fresh flowers from the garden as examples to achieve perfection in form and colour. Do not take artistic licence too literally – no decorator would, for example, change the colour of wisteria to red.

The paste used for flower petals and leaves must be of a fine texture showing no cracks caused by using a too dry modelling paste or working with too much cornflour (cornstarch) during the shaping. If wires are used, then these should be concealed where possible or if visible, covered with floristry tape.

Restraint as to the amount of **ribbon** used in a spray is advisable. Ribbon is used to complement the arrangement, not to dominate it.

Decorators contemplating exhibiting their work in competitions and shows, must **read the rules and conditions of entry** carefully, being sure to enter the exhibit in its correct class. The rules for that class must be followed exactly. Where the class reads HAND WORK ONLY all work must be executed by the decorator. Often in the conditions specific articles are permitted such as wire, tulle, ribbon, stamens and pillars; however, the use of other manufactured articles would immediately disqualify the decorator as not as schedule (N.A.S.).

Before starting the work, the decorator should again study the schedule, then plan their decorating strategies to show their skills and talents to the best advantage.

When judging a competition the judge or judges should arrive punctually at the time indicated by the show committee. If more than one judge officiates then there should be no discussion or collaboration of the work prior to judging. Each judge should assess and evaluate the exhibits in a calm and impartial manner before handing the score sheet to the steward responsible for that section.

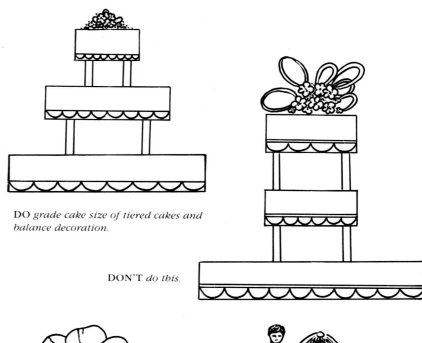

DO grade cake size of tiered cakes and balance decoration.

DON'T do this.

DON'T make moulded flowers from a dry paste that cracks.

DON'T use plastic ornaments in show work.

DON'T use too much ribbon in sprays.

DO use ribbon to complement flowers.

DO read the rules and conditions of entry carefully.

Note: It is up to the show committees to determine the type of judging they desire.

GINGERBREAD SHAPES

Children will enjoy helping you to cut out the different shapes. Tiny pieces of glacé cherry or currants can be used to decorate the shapes before they are baked.

5 ml (1 tsp) bicarbonate of soda
30 ml (2 tbsp) water
250 g (8 oz, 2 cups) plain (all-purpose) flour
large pinch of ground cloves
large pinch of ground cardamom
large pinch of ground ginger
grated rind of ½ lemon
100 g (3½ oz, ⅔ cup) blanched almonds, finely chopped
60 g (2 oz, ¼ cup) butter
220 g (7 oz, ⅔ cup) honey

Mix the bicarbonate of soda with the water and set aside. Sift the flour into a bowl with the spices, lemon rind and chopped almonds.

Melt the butter and honey together in a small pan and mix into the dry ingredients, stirring well to combine. Leave to stand for 1 hour.

Roll the gingerbread out, and cut into desired shapes. Place in a preheated oven, 180°C (350°F/Gas 4) and bake until firm and golden.

Cut the gingerbread mixture into any shape you like. If you make a hole in the top before you bake them, you can tie the baked shapes with ribbon and hang them on your Christmas tree.

75

RECIPES
CHOCOLATE CAKES

There's a cake here for everyone. Some are as easy to make as a packet mix and perfect for keen young cooks. Some are cakes to have on hand to delight family or visitors. And the layered gateaux with their lush fillings and icings make indulgent finales to grand dinner parties.

TRIPLE CHOCOLATE CAKE

15 ml (1 tbsp) white vinegar
375 ml (12 fl oz, 1½ cups) milk
280 g (9 oz, 2¼ cups) plain (all-purpose) flour
pinch of salt
90 g (3 oz, ¾ cup) cocoa powder
375 g (12 oz, 1¾ cups) caster (superfine) sugar
10 ml (2 tsp) bicarbonate of soda
250 g (8 oz, 1 cup) butter, melted and cooled
5 ml (1 tsp) vanilla essence
3 eggs, lightly beaten

Mix the vinegar and milk. Stir and leave for 15 minutes. Sift the flour, salt, cocoa powder, caster sugar and bicarbonate of soda into a large bowl. Blend in the melted butter and half the soured milk. Beat for 2 minutes. Mix in the remaining milk, vanilla essence and eggs. Beat for an extra 3 minutes. Divide the mixture evenly between 3 well greased and lined 23-cm (9-in) cake tins (pans). Bake at 180°C (350°F, Gas 4) for 30 minutes or until cooked. Leave in tins for 5 minutes before turning on to wire rack to cool. When completely cold, join the layers with **Chocolate Cream**, cover with **Chocolate Covering** and decorate with sugared violets and sweet peas.

76

Let yourself be tempted by these rich dark luscious cakes. Forget about diets, forget about will power and enjoy these cakes made with everyone's favourite flavour — chocolate. Once called 'food of the gods' and only eaten by the elite, chocolate is loved by people everywhere.

RECIPES

Chocolate Cream

250 g (8 oz, 8 squares) plain (semisweet)
chocolate, chopped
595 ml (19 fl oz, 2 cups) double (heavy)
cream

Melt the chocolate in a bowl over warm water. Heat the cream in a small pan until boiling and add slowly to the melted chocolate, stirring continually. Chill for 1 hour, then beat until thick.

Chocolate Covering

250 g (8 oz, 8 squares) plain (semisweet)
chocolate, chopped
30 ml (2 tbsp) orange-flavoured liqueur

Melt the chocolate in a bowl over warm water and beat in the liqueur.

CHOCOLATE MERINGUE CAKE

125 g (4 oz, ½ cup) unsalted butter
185 g (6 oz, ¾ cup) caster (superfine)
sugar
3 eggs, separated
90 g (3 oz, 3 squares) plain (semisweet)
chocolate, melted
100 g (3 ½ oz, 1 cup) ground almonds
60 g (2 oz, ½ cup) plain (all-purpose)
flour
5 ml (1 tsp) vanilla essence
pinch of salt
extra 30 ml (2 tbsp) caster sugar

Beat the butter and half of the sugar until creamy. Mix in the egg yolks and beat well. Blend in the chocolate, almonds, flour and remaining sugar. Beat the egg whites until soft peaks form and beat in the extra caster sugar gradually. Gently fold the egg whites into the chocolate mixture. Pour into a well greased and lined 20-cm (8-in) round cake tin (pan) and bake at 180°C (350°F, Gas 4) for 30 minutes. Leave to cool in the tin for 10 minutes before turning on to a wire rack to cool. Coat with **Chocolate Glaze**.

Chocolate Glaze

125 g (4 oz, 4 squares) plain (semisweet)
chocolate, chopped
60 g (2 oz, ¼ cup) unsalted butter
15 ml (1 tbsp) brandy

Place all the ingredients in a small bowl over warm water and stir until the chocolate melts, stirring continually.

CHERRY CHOCOLATE CAKE

250 g (8 oz, 2 cups) self-raising flour
pinch of salt
30 g (1 oz, ¼ cup) cocoa powder
5 ml (1 tsp) bicarbonate of soda
2.5 ml (½ tsp) ground cinnamon
2.5 ml (½ tsp) ground nutmeg
125 g (4 oz, ½ cup) soft butter or
margarine
125 ml (4 fl oz, ½ cup) cherry juice from
drained canned cherries
155 ml (5 fl oz, ⅔ cup) thick sour cream
2 eggs
1 egg yolk
125 g (4 oz, 1 cup) walnuts, chopped
185 g (6 oz, 1 cup) drained canned
morello cherries
extra 15 ml (1 tbsp) self-raising flour

Sift flour, salt, cocoa, bicarbonate of soda, cinnamon and nutmeg into a large mixing bowl. Add the soft butter, cherry juice and thick sour cream and beat well for 1 minute. Add eggs and egg yolk and beat for another minute. Mix the walnuts and cherries with the extra flour and fold into the cake mixture. Pour into a well greased and lined 33 × 23-cm (13 × 9-in) cake tin (pan). Bake at 180°C (350°F, Gas 4) for 45 minutes or until cooked. Leave to stand for 5 minutes before turning on to wire rack to cool. When completely cold, ice the cake with **Creamy Lemon Icing**.

Creamy Lemon Icing

60 g (2 oz, ¼ cup) butter or margarine
500 g (1 lb, 3 cups) icing (confectioner's)
sugar, sifted
15 ml (1 tbsp) grated lemon rind
15 ml (1 tbsp) lemon juice
30 ml (2 tbsp) milk

Cream the butter and beat in the icing sugar gradually. Add the lemon rind, juice and enough milk to make an icing that spreads easily.

CHERRY · CHOCOLATE ~CAKE~ with Creamy Lemon Icing

CHOCOLATE APRICOT FUDGE CAKE

250 g (8 oz, 2 cups) self-raising flour
pinch of salt
2.5 ml (½ tsp) bicarbonate of soda
125 g (4 oz, ½ cup) butter or margarine
250 g (8 oz, 1¼ cups) caster (superfine)
  sugar
90 g (3 oz, 3 squares) plain (semisweet)
  chocolate, melted
5 ml (1 tsp) vanilla essence
2 eggs, beaten
185 ml (6 fl oz, ¾ cup) milk
125 g (4 oz, ¾ cup) cooked dried apricots,
  drained and chopped

Sift together the flour, salt and bicarbonate of soda. Beat the butter and sugar together until creamy and add the beaten eggs gradually. Blend in the chocolate and vanilla essence. Add the milk alternately with the flour and stir in the chopped apricots. Pour into 2 well greased and lined 20-cm (8-in) tins (pans). Bake at 180°C (350°F, Gas 4) for 35 minutes or until cooked. Leave to stand for 5 minutes before turning on to wire rack to cool. Serve warm with **Thick Sour Cream Sauce**.

Thick Sour Cream Sauce

315 ml (10 fl oz, 1¼ cups) thick sour cream
10 ml (2 tsp) caster (superfine) sugar
10 ml (2 tsp) lemon juice
5 ml (1 tsp) vanilla essence

Mix all ingredients together.

CHOCOLATE COCONUT FUDGE CAKE

125 g (4 oz, ½ cup) butter or margarine
250 g (8 oz, 1¼ cups) caster (superfine)
  sugar
3 eggs, separated
90 g (3 oz, 3 squares) plain (semisweet)
  chocolate, melted
5 ml (1 tsp) vanilla essence
250 g (8 oz, 2 cups) self-raising flour
pinch of salt
2.5 ml (½ tsp) bicarbonate of soda
250 ml (8 fl oz, 1 cup) milk
45 g (1½ oz, ½ cup) desiccated coconut

· CHOCOLATE ·
APRICOT FUDGE
CAKE

Beat the butter and sugar until creamy. Add the egg yolks, one at a time and beat well. Blend in the chocolate and vanilla essence. Sift the flour, salt and bicarbonate of soda together and add alternately with the milk to the creamed mixture. Fold in the coconut. Beat the egg whites until stiff but not dry and fold into the chocolate mixture. Pour into 2 well greased and lined 23-cm (9-in) round cake tins (pans). Bake at 180°C (350°F, Gas 4) for 35 minutes or until cooked. Leave to stand for 5 minutes before turning on to a wire rack to cool. When completely cold ice with **Coconut Butter Frosting** and top with toasted shredded coconut.

Coconut Butter Frosting

125 g (4 oz, ½ cup) butter or margarine
500 g (1 lb, 3 cups) icing (confectioner's)
  sugar, sifted
5 ml (1 tsp) vanilla essence
1.25 ml (¼ tsp) coconut essence
45–60 ml (3–4 tbsp) milk

Cream the butter and beat in the icing sugar. Add essences and enough milk to make an icing that spreads easily.

CHOCOLATE AND HAZELNUT CAKE

155 g (5 oz, ⅔ cup) unsalted butter
280 g (9 oz, 1½ cups) caster (superfine)
  sugar
2 eggs, beaten
90 g (3 oz, 3 squares) plain (semisweet)
  chocolate, melted
5 ml (1 tsp) vanilla essence
250 g (8 oz, 2 cups) self-raising flour
pinch of salt
2.5 ml (½ tsp) bicarbonate of soda
250 ml (8 fl oz, 1 cup) milk
5 eggs, separated
extra 155 g (5 oz, ⅔ cup) caster sugar
extra 5 ml (1 tsp) vanilla essence
125 g (4 oz, ¾ cup) ground hazelnuts
10 ml (2 tsp) plain (all-purpose) flour

Beat the butter and sugar until creamy. Add the beaten eggs and mix well. Mix in the chocolate and vanilla essence. Sift the flour, salt and bicarbonate of soda together and add alternately with the milk to the creamed ingredients. Pour into 3 well greased and lined 23-cm (9-in) round cake tins (pans). Beat the egg whites until soft peaks form and gradually add half of the extra sugar. In another bowl beat the egg yolks, remaining extra sugar and the extra vanilla essence until thick. Very gently fold in the beaten egg whites. Fold in the ground hazelnuts and the plain flour. Pour the hazelnut mixture on top of the chocolate cake mixture in the tins. Bake at 180°C (350°F, Gas 4) for 35 minutes or until cooked. Leave to stand for 5 minutes before turning on to a wire rack to cool. When completely cold join cakes together with a thin layer of **Cocoa Whipped Cream** and spread the remainder all over the cake.

Cocoa Whipped Cream

500 ml (16 fl oz, 2 cups) double (thick)
  cream
100 g (3½ oz, ⅔ cup) icing
  (confectioner's) sugar
45 g (1½ oz, ⅓ cup) cocoa powder

Beat all ingredients together until thick.

CHOCOLATE RUM CAKE

Combine butter, chocolate and coffee in a bowl over warm water and stir until thoroughly blended and the chocolate melts. Cool. Beat in the sugar, eggs and vanilla essence. Sift the flour, salt and bicarbonate of soda together and add alternately with the milk to the melted chocolate mixture. Pour into 2 well greased and lined 20-cm (8-in) round cake tins (pans) and bake at 180°C (350°F, Gas 4) for 35 minutes or until cooked. Leave to stand for 5 minutes before turning on to a wire rack to cool. When completely cold, join layers with **Coffee Butter Icing** and coat with the remainder. Decorate with walnut halves.

CHOCOLATE RUM CAKE

125 g (4 oz, ½ cup) butter or margarine
345 g (11 oz, 2 cups) brown sugar
2 eggs, separated
155 g (5 oz, 1 cup) raisins, chopped
125 g (4 oz, 4 squares) plain (semisweet) chocolate, melted
60 ml (2 fl oz, ¼ cup) hot water
125 ml (4 fl oz, ½ cup) thick sour cream
315 g (10 oz, 2½ cups) self-raising flour, sifted
2.5 ml (½ tsp) mixed spice
30 ml (2 tbsp) light rum

Beat the butter and sugar together until light and fluffy. Add egg yolks and beat for 1 minute. Mix in the raisins and melted chocolate. Mix the hot water and thick sour cream together and add alternately with the flour and cinnamon to the creamed mixture. Beat egg whites until stiff but not dry and gently fold in. Pour into 2 well greased and lined 23-cm (9-in) cake tins (pans) and bake at 180°C (350°F, Gas 4) for 40 minutes or until cooked. Sprinkle with rum and allow to stand for 10 minutes before turning on to wire rack to cool. When completely cold join layers with whipped cream and ice with **Chocolate Icing**.

Chocolate Icing

30 ml (2 tbsp) single (light) cream
30 ml (2 tbsp) cocoa powder
30 ml (2 tbsp) brown sugar
5 ml (1 tsp) mixed spice
155 g (5 oz, 1 cup) icing (confectioner's) sugar, sifted

Mix together the cream, cocoa, brown sugar and mixed spice in a small pan. Heat without boiling until sugar is dissolved. Remove from heat and beat in the sifted icing sugar gradually.

MOCHA CAKE

125 g (4 oz, ½ cup) butter or margarine
60 g (2 oz, 2 squares) plain (semisweet) chocolate, chopped
125 ml (4 fl oz, ½ cup) very strong black coffee
125 g (4 oz, ½ cup) caster (superfine) sugar
2 eggs, beaten
10 ml (2 tsp) vanilla essence
250 g (8 oz, 2 cups) self-raising flour
5 ml (1 tsp) bicarbonate of soda
pinch of salt
250 ml (8 fl oz, 1 cup) milk

Coffee Butter Icing

90 g (3 oz, 1/3 cup) unsalted butter
2.5 ml (1/2 tsp) vanilla essence
250 g (8 oz, 1 1/2 cups) icing
  (confectioner's) sugar, sifted
15 – 30 ml (1 – 2 tbsp) very strong black
  coffee

Cream the butter and essence and beat in the icing sugar. Add enough of the coffee to make an icing that spreads easily.

BLACK FOREST CAKE

250 g (8 oz, 1 cup) unsalted butter
375 ml (12 fl oz, 1 1/2 cups) hot water
185 g (6 oz, 6 squares) plain (semisweet)
  chocolate, chopped
440 g (14 oz, 2 cups) caster (superfine)
  sugar
185 g (6 oz, 1 1/2 cups) plain (all-purpose)
  flour
30 g (1 oz, 1/4 cup) cocoa powder
2 large eggs, beaten
10 ml (2 tsp) vanilla essence
595 ml (19 fl oz, 2 cups) double (thick)
  cream
875 g (1 3/4 lb, 4 1/2 cups) canned
  unsweetened black cherries
60 ml (2 fl oz, 1/4 cup) kirsch

Melt the butter in a saucepan and add the hot water, chopped chocolate and caster sugar. Stir over a very low heat until the chocolate is just melted. Remove from heat and cool. Pour into a large bowl and gradually fold in the sifted flour and cocoa powder. Add the beaten eggs and vanilla essence. Pour into a deep, well greased and lined 23-cm (9-in) springform tin (pan) and bake at 160°C (325°F, Gas 3) for 1 hour or until cooked. Leave to stand for 5 minutes in pan before turning on to a wire rack to cool. When cold cut cake into 3 even layers. Sprinkle each layer with kirsch and spread with some of the whipped cream and drained cherries. Cover the cake with remaining cream and decorate with chocolate curls and cherries.

DEVIL'S FOOD CAKE

90 g (3 oz, 1/3 cup) butter or margarine
250 g (8 oz, 1 1/2 cups) brown sugar
2 eggs, beaten
125 g (4 oz, 4 squares) plain (semisweet)
  chocolate, melted
315 g (10 oz, 2 1/2 cups) plain (all-purpose)
  flour
10 ml (2 tsp) bicarbonate of soda
pinch of salt
250 ml (8 fl oz, 1 cup) milk
5 ml (1 tsp) vanilla essence

Beat the butter and sugar until light and fluffy. Add the egg gradually, beating well. Blend in the melted chocolate. Sift the flour, salt and bicarbonate of soda together and add alternately with the milk and vanilla essence to the chocolate mixture. Pour into 2 well greased and lined 20-cm (8-in) cake tins (pans) and bake at 180°C (350°F, Gas 4) for 35 minutes or until cooked. Leave to stand for 5 minutes before turning on to a wire rack to cool. When completely cold fill with **Butter Filling** and ice with **Chocolate Frosting**.

Butter Filling

90 g (3 oz, 1/3 cup) butter
185 g (6 oz, 1 cup) icing (confectioner's)
  sugar
15 ml (1 tbsp) milk

Cream the butter and gradually add the icing sugar and milk.

Chocolate Frosting

185 g (6 oz, 6 squares) plain (semisweet)
  chocolate, chopped
625 g (1 1/4 lb, 3 1/2 cups) icing
  (confectioner's) sugar, sifted
30 ml (2 tbsp) hot water
2 egg yolks
90 g (3 oz, 1/3 cup) unsalted butter, melted

Melt the chocolate in a bowl over warm water. Stir in the icing sugar and hot water and beat in the egg yolks. Beat in the melted butter very slowly.

BLACK FOREST CAKE

ICINGS AND FROSTINGS

CHOCOLATE ICING

This is superb on a rich chocolate cake

125 ml (4 fl oz, ½ cup) single (light) cream
250 g (8 oz, 8 squares) plain (semisweet)
*   chocolate*

Scald the cream in a small saucepan and add the chocolate, broken into pieces. Leave on a low heat for 1 minute, then remove the pan from the heat and stir the chocolate into the cream with a wire whisk until the chocolate has melted and the mixture is smooth.

Place the pan in a bowl of cold water to prevent the icing cooking further and leave to stand for 15 minutes, stirring occasionally before you use it.

This will generously cover the top and sides of a 23-cm (9-in) cake.

THICK SOUR CREAM ICING

250 g (8 oz, 1½ cups) icing (con-
*   fectioner's) sugar*
5 ml (1 tsp) fresh orange juice
15 ml (1 tbsp) thick sour cream
1 egg white

Sift the icing sugar into a medium-sized mixing bowl. Stir in the orange juice and thick sour cream and set aside. Beat the egg white until it forms stiff peaks and fold it into the sugar mixture until thoroughly blended and smooth. If the icing is too thick add a little more thick sour cream.

This makes enough to ice a 23-cm (9-in) cake.

CHOCOLATE GLAZE

This gives a shiny finish to rich chocolate cakes.

60 g (2 oz, 2 squares) plain (semisweet)
*   chocolate*
60 g (2 oz, ¼ cup) butter
10 ml (2 tsp) honey

Break up the chocolate and put it, with butter and honey in the top of a double boiler, or in a heatproof bowl standing over, not in, a pan of simmering water. Allow the mixture to melt, then remove the pan from the heat and beat the mixture until it is cold and begins to thicken. Pour over the top of the cake and allow to run down the sides, smoothing with a metal spatula.

Enough to coat the top and sides of a 23-cm (9-in) cake.

SIMPLE BUTTER CREAM ICING

90 g (3 oz, ⅓ cup) softened butter
500 g (1 lb, 3 cups) icing (confectioner's)
*   sugar*
45 ml (3 tbsp) single (light) cream
*   flavouring*

Cream together the butter and sugar until light and fluffy, then add the cream and continue beating until smooth. Flavourings may be 2.5 ml (½ tsp) vanilla essence or 15 ml (1 tbsp) instant coffee dissolved in 5 ml (1 tsp) Cognac, or a little orange-flavoured liqueur, or grated orange or lemon rind.

This makes enough to cover a 23-cm (9-in) cake.

CUSTARD-BASED BUTTER CREAM ICING

2 egg yolks
60 g (2 oz, ¼ cup) caster (superfine) sugar
pinch of salt
125 ml (4 fl oz, ½ cup) double (thick)
*   cream, scalded*
2.5 ml (½ tsp) vanilla essence
250 g (8 oz, 1 cup) unsalted butter

Beat the egg yolks with the sugar and salt and slowly pour over the scalded cream, stirring constantly. Put the mixture in the top part of a double boiler or into a heatproof bowl and sit it over, not in, simmering water. Cook, stirring constantly, until the mixture coats a metal spoon. Remove the pan from the heat and add the vanilla essence. Set aside until cool.

Beat the butter until it is fluffy and add it, a little at a time to the custard. You have to do this carefully, or the mixture may curdle.

You can change the flavour by adding some melted plain (semisweet) chocolate, or omit the vanilla and add a liqueur of your choice.

This will generously cover the top and sides of a 23-cm (9-in) cake.

COFFEE ICING

For a rich cream-filled layer cake.

Put 185 ml (6 fl oz, ¾ cup) very strong black coffee into a pan and add 185 g (6 oz, 1 cup) icing (confectioner's) sugar. Warm over low heat, stirring constantly and adding more icing sugar until the mixture is a heavy cream. Cool slightly and pour over the top of the cake.

A delicious way to decorate a cake covered with coffee icing is to sprinkle it thickly with finely ground pistachio nuts.

Enough for a 23-cm (9-in) cake.

CREAM CHEESE ICING

Excellent on carrot cakes

125 g (4 oz, ¾ cup) icing (confectioner's) sugar
90 g (3 oz, ⅓ cup) cream cheese
30 ml (2 tbsp) single (light) cream
7.5 ml (1½ tsp) grated lemon or orange rind

Sift the icing sugar. Beat the cream cheese with the cream until soft and fluffy. Gradually add the icing sugar, beating constantly, then the grated rind.

Enough to cover a 23-cm (9-in) cake.

BROWNED BUTTER FROSTING

Exceptionally good on carrot cake

125 g (4 oz, ½ cup) butter
625 g (1¼ lb, 3½ cups) icing (confectioner's) sugar
45 ml (3 tbsp) single (light) cream
5 ml (1 tsp) vanilla essence
30 ml (2 tbsp) grated lemon or orange rind

Heat the butter in a frying pan over moderate heat until it browns lightly. Pour the butter into a bowl and add the sugar. Beat well and stir in cream, vanilla and grated rind.

This will cover a 25-cm (10-in) cake.

PASSIONFRUIT ICING

185 g (6 oz, 1 cup) icing (confectioner's) sugar
5 ml (1 tsp) butter
pulp of 2 passionfruit

Sift the icing sugar into a bowl, add the butter and enough passionfruit pulp to mix to a stiff paste. Put the bowl over a pan of simmering water, and heat for 1 minute, stirring constantly, or until the icing has thinned a little. Remove from heat, add remaining passionfruit and spread over the top of a cake.

Enough to cover the top of a 23-cm (9-in) cake.

BUTTERSCOTCH ICING

60 g (2 oz, ¼ cup) butter
90 g (3 oz, ½ cup) brown sugar
pinch of salt
75 ml (2½ fl oz, ⅓ cup) evaporated milk
2.5 ml (½ tsp) vanilla essence

Put the butter, brown sugar, salt and evaporated milk in a bowl and stand in a pan of water over gentle heat. Alternatively, use a double boiler. Stir constantly until the butter has melted and the mixture is smooth. Remove from the heat and allow to cool slightly, then beat in the icing sugar and vanilla. You might need a little more or a little less icing sugar than stated, so don't add it all at once.

Will generously cover the top and sides of a 25-cm (10-in) cake.

PASSIONFRUIT ICING

RICH FRUIT CAKE

Two traditional fruit cake recipes which will make your cakes taste as good as they look

Enough for a two-tier wedding cake, using 25 × 25-cm (10 × 10-in) and 15 × 15-cm (6 × 6-in) cake tins (pans). The cakes should be baked about 6 weeks before the wedding to allow the flavour to mature.

625 g (1¼ lb, 2½ cups) butter
625 g (1¼ lb, 3¾ cups) brown sugar
15 ml (1 tbsp) vanilla essence
15 medium eggs
625 g (1¼ lb, 3¾ cups) sultanas (golden raisins)
625 g (1¼ lb, 3¾ cups) raisins, chopped
625 g (1¼ lb, 4 cups) currants
375 g (12 oz, 2 cups) mixed peel
200 g (6½ oz, 1¾ cups) blanched almonds, chopped
140 g (4½ oz, 1 cup) dates, chopped
140 g (4½ oz, ¾ cup) prunes, chopped
140 g (4½ oz, ¾ cup) glacé (candied) ginger, chopped
140 g (4½ oz, 1 cup) glacé cherries, cut into quarters
7.5 ml (1½ tsp) ground cinnamon
7.5 ml (1½ tsp) mixed spice
2.5 ml (½ tsp) ground nutmeg
750 g (1½ lb, 6 cups) plain (all-purpose) flour
315 ml (10 fl oz, 1¼ cups) brandy

Put all the fruit in a bowl and pour over the brandy. Cover and leave overnight.
Preheat the oven to 150°C (300°F, Gas 2). Line the baking tins with 1 layer of brown paper and 2 layers of greaseproof (wax) paper.
Cream the butter and sugar and add the vanilla essence. Add the beaten eggs one at a time, beating between each addition. Add the prepared fruit, nuts and dry ingredients and mix well. Place the mixture into the prepared tins and bake for 30 minutes. Reduce the oven heat to 140°C (275°F, Gas 1) for the remainder of the cooking time. The large cake will take approximately 5 hours, the small one approximately 3 hours. If the cake is browning too quickly, cover it with greaseproof paper halfway through the cooking time. Remove it 15 minutes before the cake is ready. Remove the cake from the oven and while it is still warm, wrap the tin and cake in a large towel until it is cool.

This recipe will make a 20-cm (8-in) round cake or an 18-cm (7-in) square cake.

500 g (1 lb, 3 cups) currants
185 g (6 oz, 1 cup) sultanas (golden raisins)
185 g (6 oz, 1 cup) raisins, chopped
60 g (2 oz, ⅓ cup) glacé (candied) cherries, chopped
60 g (2 oz, ⅓ cup) mixed peel, chopped
45 ml (3 tbsp) brandy
250 g (8 oz, 2 cups) plain (all-purpose) flour
2.5 ml (½ tsp) salt
1.25 ml (¼ tsp) freshly grated nutmeg
2.5 ml (½ tsp) ground cinnamon
60 g (2 oz, ½ cup) blanched almonds, chopped
250 g (8 oz, 1½ cups) brown sugar
10 ml (2 tsp) black treacle (molasses)
250 g (8 oz, 1 cup) unsalted butter
4 eggs
grated rind of 1 lemon and 1 orange

Put all the fruit in a bowl and pour over the brandy. Cover and leave overnight.
Preheat the oven to 140°C (275°F, Gas 1). Grease the cake tin and line it with greaseproof (wax) paper.
Cream the butter and sugar together until light and fluffy. Beat the eggs and add them, a tablespoon at a time, to the creamed mixture, beating well after each addition. Add a little flour if the mixture starts to curdle. When all the eggs have been added, fold in the sifted flour and spices. Add the fruit, nuts, treacle and grated fruit rinds. Mix well. Spoon the mixture into the prepared cake tin and spread it out evenly with the back of a spoon. Tie a band of brown paper around the outside of the tin and cover the top of the cake with a double square of greaseproof paper with a hole cut in the centre. Bake near the bottom of the oven for 4½ – 4¾ hours. Test with a skewer. Remove from the oven, cool the cake in its tin, in a towel and store in an airtight container.

84

RECIPES
ROYAL ICING

Royal icing is used for pipework with all sized tubes, from the finest to the largest. It is also broken down with water and used for floodwork (see page 59).

Unless the correct consistency is achieved in the mixing, difficulties may occur, especially when using the finer tubes. It is only after preparing several batches of this mixture that the novice will gain the necessary judgement and skill to produce a satisfactory working medium with the appropriate consistency. To achieve success in this regard is of the utmost importance and experience is the ultimate teacher.

The following points must be observed:

1. The egg white used must be fresh and at room temperature.

2. The icing (confectioner's) sugar *must* be pure and finely sifted.

3. When adding the sugar gradually to the egg white, it is always wise to beat each addition very well, particularly in the early stages. A steady circular movement with a wooden spoon or metal spatula is the best method of beating; it is not good enough just to stir.

4. A drop or two of acetic acid will give cohesion to the egg white and produce a lightness to the royal icing. But overuse of this acid will cause drying and produce a brittle mixture when piping. When adding it to the mixture, use an eyedropper.

Royal icing recipe

1 egg white, at room temperature
approximately 250 g (8 oz, 1½ cups) icing
(confectioner's) sugar, sifted
1 drop of acetic acid

1. Place the egg white in a small glass or china mixing bowl. Make sure the bowl and equipment for use have been washed and dried and are perfectly clean, to ensure an optimum result.

2. Add 30 ml (2 tbsp) icing sugar and beat well until it has thoroughly combined with the egg white. This will take 2–3 minutes of hand beating.

3. Continue to add the sugar, reducing it now to 15 ml (1 tbsp) at a time. Beat well between each addition until the mixture has a syrupy consistency and maintains a smoothness and gloss throughout the beating.

4. Add the acetic acid. Continue to add icing sugar 5 ml (1 tsp) at a time, beating well between each addition, until the mixture reaches a 'soft peak' or 'lattice' consistency.

This stage is reached when the royal icing peaks on the back of the spoon. When the spoon is reversed, the peak will stand erect, then tilt to a 45° angle. This consistency is used for writing, dots, lattice, embroidery, tulle work, bridgework (drop lines) and lace.

The 'firm peak' stage is achieved by beating a little extra sugar into the mixture. The peak should stand smooth, tapered and erect on the back of the spoon. This consistency is used for shell border work and piped flowers.

Note: Decorators who have 'hot' hands may need to alter these guideline stages to suit themselves.

To fill the icing bag

Small paper cone
1. First form a circle with the thumb and index finger of the left hand (or right hand, if left-handed).

2. Place the bag, point first, through the circle until the shape of the cone fits comfortably in the hole formed by the fingers. The flap of the bag, which has been tucked into the cone to secure the bag, should be placed top-side to the index finger and not resting on the thumb.

3. Using a small spatula or a knife take a small amount of royal icing from the container or bowl, insert the blade into the paper cone with the icing facing downward towards the thumb. Use the thumb as a pressure point to wipe the icing from the knife and into the bag.

4. Repeat this process until the bag is half to three-quarters full before removing the cone from the finger circle.

5. To fold the bag, turn a fold approximately 1-cm (½-in) wide from the right-hand top-side towards the centre, then another the same width from the left-hand side towards the centre. Then fold the peak at the back of the bag over to the front and continue folding until the icing is firmly enclosed within a well-sealed piping bag which should remain firm and compact throughout its use. To accomplish this, it is necessary to continually 'fold in' as required.

Positioning the bag for use
1. The small bag is held in a similar way to a pen or pencil for writing. The difference is that the thumb is lifted from the side of the bag and placed directly to the top. The thumb is the main pressure control used to force the royal icing through the small aperture in the point.

Note: A well-made bag should have a sharp clean point from which no icing flows until just prior to use when the point is cut to size with a pair of scissors.

Tubes are more successfully used in the medium and large bags whereas the small cone is very efficient for fine to medium pipework or it can produce an excellent royal icing leaf by flattening the point of the filled bag between the fingers and cutting a small, even-mitred point.

Medium and large bags
1. Before filling the bags with royal icing, cut sufficient from the pointed tip to allow approximately 1 cm (½ in) of the tube to protrude, once inserted inside the bag.

2. Hold the paper cone, gently yet firmly in the left hand (or if left-handed, right hand). Lift a scoop of royal icing from the bowl with a wooden spoon or spatula and shake it into the open bag.

3. Repeat this process until the bag is half full. Fold both sides of the top of the bag in towards the centre as previously described for the small cone and fold the top peak at the back of the bag over the front, enclosing the royal icing. Continue to fold and tuck until the icing is well sealed within and ready for use.

4. The bag should remain firmly compact throughout its use by continuous 'folding in'.

Positioning the bag for use
1. Fully open the hand and lay the bag diagonally across the palm with the tube end extending towards the small finger. The top should fit snugly under the thumb.

2. Close the hand by wrapping the four fingers around the bag, then lower the thumb over the top folded position of the bag and gently squeeze until the icing flows from the tube.

3. When not in use, place the tube end under a damp cloth or in a stand over a damp piece of sponge foam.

FRUIT CAKE
TIN SIZE CHART

If you have ever wondered how to adjust your favourite recipes to fit into different size cake tins, the following chart will help. It gives a recipe for a delicious fruit cake with different quantities of ingredients for different size tins.

The quantities given in the following chart will fill one 7.5-cm (3-in) deep cake tin of the size stated. The tins need to be lined and any pudding basin or mixing bowl used for baking must be ovenproof. The method of mixing is the same for all sizes.

CAKE TIN (PAN) SIZES	13-cm (5-in) round	13-cm (5-in) square; 15-cm (6-in round); 1-litre (32-fl oz, 4-cup) pudding basin	15-cm (6-in) square; 18-cm (7-in) round	18-cm (7-in) square; 20-cm (8-in) round; 2-litre (4-pint, 8-cup) pudding basin; 25 × 18 × 7.5-cm (10 × 7 × 3-in) rectangle	20-cm (8-in) square; 23-cm (9-in) round	23-cm (9-in) square; 25-cm (10-in) round; 25 × 20 × 7.5-cm (10 × 8 × 3-in) rectangle
INGREDIENTS						
Butter or margarine	90 g (3 oz, ⅓ cup)	100 g (3½ oz, ⅓ cup)	155 g (5 oz, ⅔ cup)	185 g (6 oz, ¾ cup)	280 g (9 oz, 1⅓ cups)	375 g (12 oz, 1½ cups)
Brown sugar	90 g (3 oz, ⅓ cup)	100 g (3½ oz, ½ cup)	155 g (5 oz, 1 cup)	185 g (6 oz, 1 cup)	280 g (9 oz, 1¾ cups)	375 g (12 oz, 2¼ cups)
Eggs	2	2	3	3	4	6
Plain (all-purpose) flour	100 g (3½ oz, ½ cup)	155 g (5 oz, 1 cup)	170 g (5½ oz, 1 cup)	220 g (7 oz, 1⅓ cups)	345 g (11 oz, 2¾ cups)	440 g (14 oz, 3½ cups)
Salt	pinch	pinch	pinch	2.5 ml (½ tsp)	2.5 ml (½ tsp)	2.5 ml (½ tsp)
Mixed spice	2.5 ml (½ tsp)	5 ml (1 tsp)	5 ml (1 tsp)	7.5 ml (1½ tsp)	10 ml (2 tsp)	20 ml (4 tsp)
Raisins	100 g (3½ oz, ½ cup)	155 g (5 oz, 1 cup)	220 g (7 oz, 1⅓ cups)	315 g (10 oz, 1½ cups)	440 g (14 oz, 2⅔ cups)	625 g (1¼ lb, 3¾ cups)
Currants	75 g (2½ oz, ⅓ cup)	100 g (3½ oz, ⅔ cup)	155 g (5 oz, 1 cup)	170 g (5½ oz, 1¼ cups)	220 g (7 oz, 1½ cups)	345 g (11 oz, 2⅓ cups)
Sultanas (golden raisins)	75 g (2½ oz, ½ cup)	100 g (3½ oz, ½ cup)	170 g (5½ oz, 1 cup)	220 g (7 oz, 1⅓ cups)	345 g (11 oz, 2 cups)	440 g (14 oz, 2½ cups)
Glacé (candied) cherries	45 g (1½ oz, ¼ cup)	45 g (1½ oz, ¼ cup)	45 g (1½ oz, ¼ cup)	60 g (2 oz, ⅓ cup)	75 g (2½ oz, ½ cup)	155 g (5 oz, 1⅓ cups)
Flaked almonds	15 g (½ oz, 2 tbsp)	30 g (1 oz, ¼ cup)	30 g (1 oz, ¼ cup)	45 g (1½ oz, ⅓ cup)	45 g (1½ oz, ⅓ cup)	75 g (2½ oz, ½ cup)
Grated lemon rind	1.25 ml (¼ tsp)	2.5 ml (½ tsp)	2.5 ml (½ tsp)	5 ml (1 tsp)	5 ml (1 tsp)	7.5 ml (1½ tsp)
OVEN TEMPERATURE	140°C (275°F, Gas 1)	140°C (275°F, Gas 1)	140°C (275°F, Gas 1)	140°C (275°F, Gas 1)	140°C (275°F, Gas 1)	140°C (275°F, Gas 1)
COOKING TIME (approx)	1½ hours	1½ – 2 hours	2 hours	3 – 3½ hours	3½ – 4 hours	4 – 4½ hours

Method

Cream the butter and brown sugar in a mixing bowl until light and fluffy. Beat in the eggs, one at a time. Sift the flour, salt and mixed spice together and then fold gently into the creamed butter and sugar mixture. Add the remaining ingredients to the bowl and stir well until thoroughly mixed. Do not overbeat. Turn into the prepared cake tin and smooth the top. Make a very small dip in the centre of the cake to help it rise more evenly. Bake the cake in a slow oven until cooked. Test by inserting a thin skewer in the centre of the cake. If it comes out without raw cake adhering to it, the cake is cooked. Remove from oven immediately and wrap cake in an old blanket or several towels so that it cools slowly. Leave to become quite cold before removing from the tin.

TIPS

Here are the solutions to some of the problems which worry cake decorators, particularly those who have not had much experience. You will find that they will really help you to achieve better results easily.

WINTER 8 min

SUMMER 5 min

LIGHT CAKES IN WINTER, HEAVY IN SUMMER

If you find you make light cakes in the winter and heavy ones in the summer, it could be that you are over-beating your butter and sugar in the hot weather. In the winter creaming takes about 7 or 8 minutes of beating until the mixture is thick and creamy and in the summer it will take less time.

Other causes of heavy cakes could be too low or too high oven temperature or too much beating when adding the flour and milk. And just to make it difficult for the beginner, the under-mixing of the flour and milk will also cause a heavy cake. Batter must be beaten until smooth after each addition of flour and milk, but not too much!

STOP FRUIT SINKING

If you want to stop fruit or nuts sinking to the bottom of light fruit cakes during baking, take a little of the flour in the recipe and mix it with the fruit or nuts before adding to the cake batter. Over-sugared crystallized cherries need rinsing and drying before flouring.

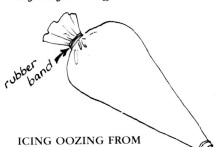

rubber band

ICING OOZING FROM PIPING BAG

If you have the problem of royal icing oozing out of the top of the piping bag as you work, twist a rubber band on after filling to stop this happening.

UNEVEN LAYER CAKES

If you find you are still getting uneven baking in your layer cakes no matter how carefully you spread the batter in the tins, the problem is usually uneven heating in your oven. The solution could be to bake one cake at a time in the centre of the rack.

STICKING PAPER TO A BASE BOARD

If you find you are out of adhesive when you want to glue paper to a base board, make your own by dissolving one teaspoon of gelatine in a cup of warm water.

STICKING SUGARPASTE TO A BASE BOARD

If you are covering a base board with sugarpste (fondant), use egg white to 'glue' it.

FOOD COLOURINGS

Paste colours are generally the best to use for colouring royal icing or sugarpaste. They are glycerine-based and come in a good colour range. Add the colour to the icing with a cocktail stick (toothpick).

NOVELTY TINS

If you do not know how much cake mixture you will need, fill a cake tin you have used many times with water to the top. Pour the water into the new tin. This will give you a good idea of how much mixture to make.

IF YOUR BUTTER CAKES HAVE A 'HILL' IN THE MIDDLE

It could be you have added too much flour, or overbeaten the batter or not spread the uncooked cake to the sides of the tin so that there is a slight depression in the centre before the cake is baked.

"THE NUMBER ONE MANUFACTURER OF QUALITY HAND TOOLS"

ODENSE
·MARCIPANFABRIK·

The world's best range of almond products
from PURATOS...who else?

Renshaw
QUALITY FOODS

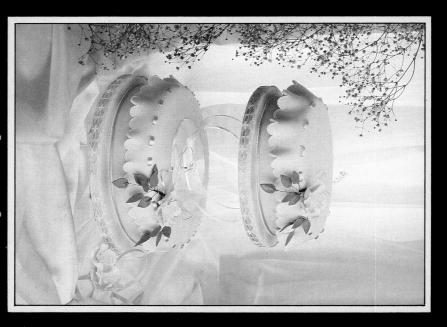

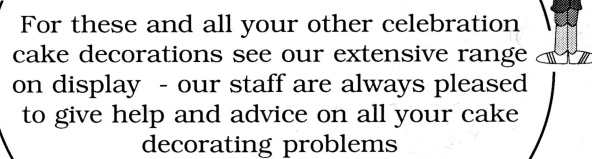

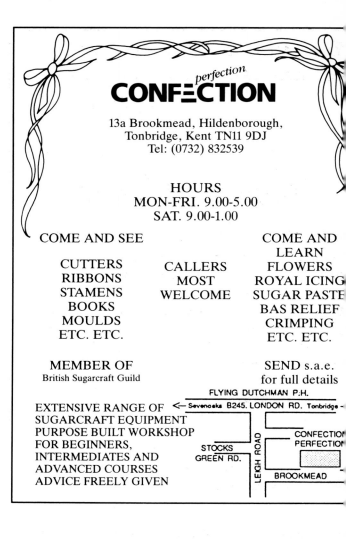

MEREHURST

The Cake Decorating Specialists

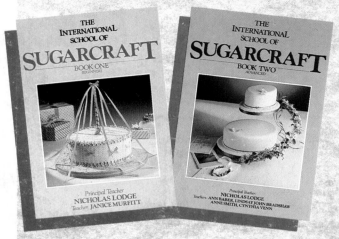

INTERNATIONAL SCHOOL OF SUGARCRAFT
BOOK I & BOOK II

Principal Teacher: Nicholas Lodge

Britain's top sugarcraft artists share their secrets in these two volumes, each containing twenty lessons and together forming a complete course in cake decoration.

PATTERNS FOR CAKE DECORATING

Lindsay John Bradshaw

For a really professional finish this is an invaluable reference source with 500 actual size templates which can be traced off the page. Also by the same author, STENCILLING FOR CAKE DECORATING and LETTERING FOR CAKE DECORATING.

FINISHING TOUCHES

A world best seller, covering all the essentials of cake decorating, from the basics of sugarpaste and royal icing to the most elaborate of sugar flower sprays.

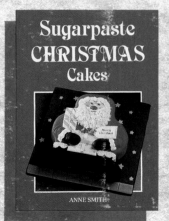

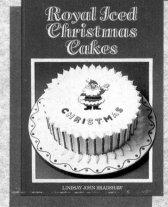

SUGARPASTE CHRISTMAS CAKES

Anne Smith

ROYAL ICED CHRISTMAS CAKES

Lindsay John Bradshaw

Original and varied designs for cakes for the festive season.